What Is So Good About Getting Older

Another Way of Looking At Aging

Written by

Dr. Ronald G. Sherman

authorHOUSE®

AuthorHouse™
1663 Liberty Drive, Suite 200
Bloomington, IN 47403
www.authorhouse.com
Phone: 1-800-839-8640

First published by AuthorHouse 6/30/2008

ISBN: 978-1-4343-8582-6 (e)
ISBN: 978-1-4343-8581-9 (sc)

Library of Congress Control Number: 2008905658

Printed in the United States of America
Bloomington, Indiana

This book is printed on acid-free paper.

Acknowledgments

Many people contributed to this book. First of all I want to thank God, who is known by many names to many people. Thank you for sending me some of your angels who seem to always be around when I need them and even when I think I do not. Without your constant inspiration and guidance this book may never have come to fruition.

I would like to especially thank Cynthia who again turned my thoughts into complete sentences. To the many patients whom over the years have contributed their opinions and advice in the formulation of this book. Thank you to Dodie who gave her viewpoints on some difficult questions. Thank you to Pat and John for your encouragement and inspiration. Thank you to my colleagues for their ongoing support. And lastly of course a deep sense of gratitude to my wife Pamela, and children; Keith, Evan and Sean. You again have shown great patience with my idiosyncrasies. The adventure continues.

Introduction

Who was that person who coined the phrase "The Golden Years," because I would like to have a discussion with him/her about that definition and perception of aging?

I have been in the medical profession for over 33 years, previously as a Chiropractor and currently as a Physical Therapist. For most of my career I have been working in the geriatric field. Unfortunately the patients I see are not in the best of health. My perspective on the golden years is that they are not so Golden.

In speaking with thousands of patients through the years I have listened to them and observed that these individuals were not experiencing the

"Golden years." Let us take the adventure of aging and look at the senior years from both a positive and negative perception. Listen to our seniors and find out what is golden if at all about aging.

My patients' responses "What is so great about the golden years?" are found below.

What is so Golden about aging? The answer is "NOTHING is golden about it." I have engaged my patients in conversation to learn about them as unique individuals, not just as patients with ailments. I have listened to their viewpoints and came to my own conclusions. I am currently considered an early senior citizen and with a membership to AARP. As of the writing of this book, I am 57 years old with a perspective not too far behind my patients.

This book is a follow up to my first book "Faith, Confidence and Belief." I hope the reader receives a positive viewpoint on the aging process. As I have mentioned many times to my patients and in my book, words are very powerful. Perception is reality. My desire in writing these books is the adage that *words are food for thought. Your brain works like a computer observing what goes in and reflecting what comes out. If you put junk in then junk will come out.*

The words (food for thought) in this book are my opinions and perceptions. I with a desire to look at oneself as they age and appreciate the process with a hardy sense of humor and deep gratitude to the almighty for giving them the gift of life. With this gift given to us, we have the free will to do as we choose and to live life (good or bad, right or wrong). Enjoy the experience and never stop appreciating the gift given to us. The adventure is ours to create. Let the adventure begin and let us journey into the Golden years with an open mind to various opinions, perceptions from our seniors, and ourselves.

The Aging Process Defined

According to AARP you are considered a senior citizen at 50 years. I divided the senior experience into three categories; a) early (young) senior citizen ages 50 through 65, b) middle age senior citizen age 66 through 80, and late (old) senior citizen ages 81 through 100. Since more and more people are living past 100, I came up with a new category. I think if someone makes it to 100 years old they should start over. Let's call 100 and above adolescent senior citizens with ages 39 and holding.

The aging process starts at conception. Most men reach their cell plateau at 21 and women at 25. More cells in your body are dying than being created so essentially you are losing cells past this point rather than gaining more cells. Except if you are a male and balding than all bets are off and you have more cells leaving than coming. I happen to be bald and can attest to that fact.

Look at the aging process with regard to the three points, as I call them, of our make up. Picture a triangle with one point on top and two points on the bottom. The two points on the bottom lead to the one point on top. Put the physical aspect of your life on the left bottom position, the emotional aspect of your life on the right bottom, and the spiritual aspect of your life at the top position. It is my viewpoint that this triangle should be equal in all angles. Assuming this equality, our lives should be a balance between the physical, emotional, and spiritual. We strive as a species for this balance (harmony) on a day-to-day basis. Unfortunately in my opinion this balance is not achieved as often as we would like.

In our early years we are unbalanced in that the physical and emotional aspects are far greater than the spiritual even though, depending on your religious preferences, religious school education was probably given to us. Remember as a teenager religious education was present but attending the dances, concerts, hanging out with friends, and puberty were probably taking front stage instead of religion and spirituality.

At age 20 to 30 we probably were married and some of us had children. Oh where did the time go? We were so busy with just taking care of our family, working hard raising our children, and once in a while taking a vacation the triangle was unbalanced. The physical and emotional aspects again are dominating the scene. We are aware of our spirituality but the kids have to get to soccer practice, basketball practice, or cheer leading rehearsals. By the time we return home, we hit the sofa and fall asleep only to awaken to another day of physical and emotional attention. Yes we do go to Church or Synagogue one day a week and on special days, but for the most part we are engaged in the day-to-day routine of raising our kids and attending meetings.

We made it through age 30 and now we have the age 40 to 50's to look forward to. Our kids have grown so fast making some of us grandparents. The alarm clock rings and we are off to work again so we can pay for those previous years. Some of us are more fortunate in that we have the choice to retire early, but the alarm clock still rings and off to work we go. My point here is that the triangle is still unbalanced with the physical and emotional aspects getting far more attention than the spiritual aspect. At this point we are beginning to feel some of the wonderful effects of living under a gravity planet. In other words slight aches and pains are now popping up and we are a little stiffer in the morning.

I was an athlete in my younger days and a pretty good running back. One day when my older son was playing high school football I told him that I was pretty fast in my day. Now here comes the challenge. My son says, "Oh yeah old man I could have beat you in a race." This is the challenge that goes on in all aspects of life on this planet. The young buck challenging the older buck. Well being an ex-athlete I was not going to let this challenge go unanswered. I responded back to my son, "I can beat you NOW in a race." Well put up or shut up the race was on.

My son was 17 years old at the time and I was 48. We lined up in the street and my younger son said, "On your mark set go," and we were off. The one problem to this event happened;

my legs did not get the same signal that my mind sent out. Out of the gate my son took off and I tumbled to the ground. My son was used to doing sprints and my last sprint was many years ago. It was as if I forgot how to run. I did not accept defeat; my ego would not allow that, so we lined up again. This time I concentrated on leaving the block correctly. We heard the instruction, ready, set, go. This time I left the starting block and ran with all my gusto and I lost but not by much. The next day I couldn't walk. The pain in my calves was pretty painful. I went to my doctor and we had x-rays taken. There were no fractures or torn ligaments - just a bad sprain/strain. I was on crutches for 3 weeks with a diagnosis of bruised ego. At this point in my life my mind said I can still run like the wind but my body said, "OH REALLY." The end result was that my body won out. These are the 40 to 50 years. The physical starts waning but the emotional is running well. My ego said I can still run like the wind but the reality was I could NOT.

If you are fortunate to be healthy (no major diseases or ailments) you cruise through these years but still not the same as the previous category (20 through 30's). Many diseases begin to show themselves at this juncture but you may have enough reserve energy to hide most of the symptoms. If you are not so fortunate then these diseases start their process ever so subtlety and keep growing in awareness. Those problems don't seem to go away. When one is so busy at work who has the time to give in to those ailments.

Now we discuss ages 60 to 70. At this point our mortality is making its appearance. Now our spirituality is being considered. Our physical aspect is steadily declining. Our emotional aspect is holding its own. Many of our discussions with our peers are in regard to Medicare benefits and medical costs and our ailments. Our egos have settled down.

I don't think that I can still get on the football field and compete. Any competition will be in the senior Olympics. Even Jack LaLane has changed his workouts. Let's face it our bodies are feeling the effects of gravity. We are sagging, everything is going south. We look forward to those naps. Our egos are suggesting we remember when we tried to run rather than "I can do that." The No's are winning out.

Let's face it, we are slowing down physiologically, and mentally. I am not in that

decade yet but I am quickly approaching. Compared to the next decade of 80 to 90's the 60 to 70's look pretty good. It is kind of funny when I am in a group of people older than I am, let's say in there 70's, I am considered just a youngster. However, when I am in a group of people in their 30's I am considered an old man. Yet, I am still the same age in both groups. The difference is their perception. Like I said earlier perception is your reality. Is that glass of water half filled or half empty?

Meet The Players

The following is a story about Dodie. Dodie is an attractive, very pleasant, mid seventies female who has demonstrated fantastic responses to physical therapy treatment. When I first met Dodie she was essentially bedridden/ wheelchair bound from pelvic fractures and advanced arthritis. She had been a resident in the nursing facility for several weeks at the time I met her. Her physical therapy program was emphasizing strengthening, but it appeared she was beginning to plateau and the current gains were what they were.

I took over her case and started working on various activities to strengthen her legs, trunk, and neck muscles. Dodie was not able to keep her head in an erect position due to pain and advanced arthritis. This impairment made it very difficult for her to sit for any length of time let alone entertain the idea of standing.

My approach to physical therapy intervention is looking at the triangle analogy (the physical, emotional and spiritual). My examination/ assessment did reveal the same findings as my predecessors, but one must look at the spiritual component as well. In front of me was a mid 70's senior citizen with postural ailments showing the devastating effects of arthritis. Also in front of me was an individual made up of over 45 quadrillion cells organized into several highly complex organs with a circulatory system longer in distance than the USA, a brain that handles millions of messages compartmentalizing them into sight sound memories and instructions to arms, legs, organs and thoughts.

All of these actions are held together by an organ so vast and pliable called our skin, a unique temple housing the image of God in our spirituality. This was quite an advanced picture as compared to just the physical findings the physical therapy examination revealed. Understanding that complex picture is what we work with when we begin to treat our patients. It is that perception I brought to the table when I began to work with Dodie.

At first Dodie told me she had not walked in several months, had not been able to hold her head erect, and had not been able to stand or bring her legs on or off the bed. I asked her if she was enjoying the Golden years. Her response was "Are you kidding?" Physical therapy continued on a daily basis and you can guess what happened. Dodie initially required maximal assistance to transfer her from lying in bed to sitting on the edge of the bed. Then maximal assistance was needed to go from sitting on the edge of the bed to standing and pivoting to the wheelchair. It was hard and each phase was a little bit harder than the previous one. Progress was slow and steady. Then one day I made the bold statement, "You will walk by the end of the week," Dodie. The look I got from her was one of are you crazy? Well maybe a little. Towards the end of the week I brought Dodie into the gym and placed her inside of the parallel bars. We stood up and with all her inner strength she took 5 steps. All along I knew she would walk again and it was the image that I kept in my brain every time I worked with her. I stayed within the parameters of Faith,Confidence and Belief. We added enthusiasm/excitement and certainly action. Dodie did everything I asked her to do. The results were coming. Dodie continued to make progress and is currently walking greater than 250 feet with a walker and supervision.

Dodie also steadily improved with her neck position and her transfer skills. In fact, at the time of this writing she had moved back into her apartment. Dodie now comes into the center as an outpatient. I asked Dodie what is so good about aging. At first she mentioned how hard it was to do any of the physical activities due to the arthritis. From the physical perspective, nothing is good about the aging process. Then I asked Dodie about the emotional component. Well, I know I am in my seventies but in my mind I kind of feel a lot younger than that. My memories are not as crisp as they use to be. I asked her how far back she can go in her memories. A smile came across her face as she began to describe a scene with her mother in it… "I was a little girl, maybe 5 or six, I was wearing a printed dress." Dodie went on in describing the scene in more detail and the smile continued. I gathered from her expression that this was a pleasant memory.

I continued to ask, "What then is good, if anything, about aging." Pausing for a moment she said, "Getting to see my children grow and have children of their own is well worth the pain I go through. To see my grandson grow up, and to be part of children and grandchildren's lives is worth it." Yes, that part of aging is Golden. Dodie is a person whose religious beliefs are a vital part of her life.

Even though I have a different interpretation about religious tenets we were able to communicate without ending up fighting. Isn't that one of the major tenets of our great country "Religious Freedom." We began to discuss spirituality. I explained my viewpoint regarding the triangle (physical, emotional, and spiritual) and that all roads lead to the spiritual. I continued to explain my perception that as the physical wanes with age the emotional kind of holds its own, but the spiritual begins to open with the aging process. It is that door opening that makes aging Golden.

Dodie explained her viewpoint that the miracle of life is given to us from God and it is our duty to honor his gift. I asked, "Is getting older an honor given to you from God?" Dodie replied, "In a way yes." When I asked, "Would you consider that to be within the realm of the expression the Golden years"? Dodie replied, "Well, from a spiritual perspective yes." One good thing about aging is the further opening of our spiritual aspect.

So what's so good about aging? Your spirituality takes front stage. The who you really are comes into the forefront. It is kind of like a door opening up and answers are being made clear to you. Knowing, from my book "Faith Confidence and Belief", the E of the formula is critical. The E represents enthusiasm and excitement. This component is critical to make the formula work. I asked Dodie what she was excited about. Her response was quick, "watching my children grow." I asked Dodie, "Is that a good thing about aging"? Her answer was not so quick. A few moments later she said, "I guess it does."

What else can you think of that would be categorized as good in the aging process, I asked her. The experiences/memories, not all good but for the most part I can choose which ones I will think about. Dodie said, "Yes those are good things about aging."

Now we are going to meet Bill and Mary. When I first opened my practice in Longword, Florida one of my first patients was a very pleasant, elderly, couple Bill and Mary. I was their Doctor as well as their friend. Mary was very much into her spirituality and Bill was very much into woodworking. I visited their home several times and got to know them fairly well. Mary was very open to various viewpoints regarding spiritual concerns, but pretty set on her own perception of how God keeps us humans in line. Bill helped me set up my office and even built me an examining table. Our conversations were up-to-date within the scientific world, health world, and political world basically, any every day topic I would have with any of my peers.

That is the point I am making here. Even though Mary and Bill were well over 30 years older than I, I never thought of them as anything other than my friends (contemporaries). I rarely thought that they were of another generation (my parents' age) and welcomed them into my life as friends regardless of their age. I was privileged to have met this couple as they shared some very inspirational viewpoints and common wisdom that helped me in my business and in my spiritual growth. They were good friends that entered my life when I needed good friends. I am sure they felt similar to my perception regardless of my age or title. So here we have an elderly couple and a 30 year old professional meeting on common ground called friendship. I was fortunate to have them as friends and I am sure they felt the same way. We shared our life's experiences at that particular moment in time regardless of the age differences. Isn't that a good thing about aging?

This reminds me of an old adage; "When the student is ready the teacher will appear and when the teacher is ready the student will appear.?

One of my many options in the field is doing home healthcare. This is where I visit the patients' homes to treat rather than having them come to the clinic. I remember several patients I visited and being the conversationalists they shared several stories about their lives.

Another patient told me a story of how her father would take her to the fair. At one particular fair, they were offering rides in a biplane. Her father paid the 25 cents and my patient was secured to her seat and off they went. The interesting thing about this particular ride is the pilot's name. My patient paused, and with a sparkle in her eyes she told me the name of that particular pilot, a young man by the name of Charles Lindberg. History tells us the famous story of this brave young pilot. My patient brushed up with history and she was very proud that she could remember this wonderful experience and to live to tell me and probably many others that she took a ride in an airplane piloted by Charles Lindberg. I believe this can be put down on the side of good things about aging.

One day I was working with another elderly patient in her home and the conversation led us to what she was doing to keep herself busy. My patient began to tell me that her father was a fighter pilot in world war one. She said her father didn't really talk too much about those experiences but told her his story about a dog fight. My patient went on to tell me that her father shot down the famous "Red Baron" of WWI fame. She said that her research was going forward and she was working on a book telling the story about her father. Whether this story is true or not, you had to see the gleam in her eyes when she shared the project with me.

Passing on stories from our past is an age old tradition. I certainly recommend each of us record OUR STORIES, so the next generation can have some insight into who we were and where we came from. The past is one of the solid foundations upon the building of your life's history. I realize that not all past experiences are pleasant; many are sad and painful. The beautiful thing about those memories is that for the most part you can choose which ones to think about. I understand that this is not always true and thank goodness we have highly trained psychological professionals to help us deal with those thoughts.

In our society youth is emphasized a lot more than geriatrics. It is going to be very interesting to observe how our advertisers pitch their products. Will they pitch them mainly to the youth of our nation, or will they pitch them to the aging population, the baby boomers? I am a part of the baby boomer generation and my generation makes up the majority of people in the country. For the most part, we are still working and contributing to the economy by paying taxes and purchasing products. I do not mean that our seniors are not contributing to society. They pay taxes and purchase products as well as the younger generations.

I am working with an elderly lady who happens to be essentially bedridden. She tells me that just a few months ago she was walking around, and living independently in her own apartment. She used a cane for support to help her with an arthritic knee. Somehow this knee became infected and the infection spread throughout her body. When I met her she could not walk or even get out of bed. The pain was too intense. In fact it was painful wherever she was touched. We call this being tactile defensive.

This problem made working with her within the parameters of physical therapy very difficult. Being the chronic optimist, I persevered and each day I would share with her some positive physiological property about her body. Each day I gave her a pep talk, as my patients would describe it. I never gave up the pray that she would get better. We tried several techniques to no avail. Then one day my patient told me she moved a certain way and heard a "pop sound" in her painful knee. I examined her knee and found nothing indicating that any new problems were present.

Prior to this event my patient was getting more "depressed" about her dilemma. She was losing hope in spite of my daily pep talks. The amazing thing about this pop sound is that my patient started to respond in a positive way to all the techniques that were done. I don't know why her knee popped at that particular time but apparently it happened. Whether her knee moved into a different position, or an adhesion released is not the point. It happened without any further pathology occurring. I observed no difference in her knee after the sound. Her knee looked the same; the range of motion was the same. The interesting sequence of events was that she started to walk. Her perception of something happening was true to her. This bedridden senior patient eventually walked out of the nursing facility and returned to her own home living an independent life style.

Does it matter how a miracle appears? When the student is ready the teacher appears. I received a very nice card from her telling me how grateful she is for those daily pep talks and the care from the entire staff in helping her return to a normal independent lifestyle.

In looking at the triangle model the physical aspect took a hit. Not so Golden. But through perseverance hope was not abandoned. With Faith, Confidence, and Belief, an underlying enthusiasm accompanied by action of our part a result was attained. This patient experienced a unique occurrence. She physically got ill but she physically got well.

You ask what is so good about aging? Here is an example of the deterioration of the physical but a restoration of that same physical. Ed was admitted to our skilled nursing facility in the fall. We had to get an extra large bed and wheelchair because Ed was quite obese. Ed was also bedridden and had very arthritic knees. The doctors had told him that he would probably never walk again. Ed at this point could not go home and was faced the possibility that his remaining years would be in our nursing facility. The Golden years were not so Golden. In fact, they were pretty bad. We started working with Ed with his mobility and strength concerns.

Ed was a religious man and his prayers were not being answered at this time. Again hope was diminishing. My explanations were not helping Ed. We all continued to have Faith, Confidence, and Belief. The process works, because God makes no junk.

The pieces began to fall into place. Ed was slowly taken through a progression of interventions that started him to gradual weight bearing. Then came the day when he stood up in the parallel bars for the first time. With a lot of courage and faith Ed stood. As the weeks progressed Ed was walking within the parallel bars. I guess at this time the Golden years were looking better. Ed made it home where he set up a gym to help him gain more strength. He did walk again. The tears of joy were contagious when Ed left. Ed said he had never experienced such a series of events as what he went through. I guess we don't stop benefiting from God's blessings no matter how old we are.

While working with an elderly patient doing home healthcare in Central Florida one particular patient was the oldest patient I have ever worked with. She was 106 years old. I asked her the proverbial question, "What do you attribute your long life to?" She said, "I don't cuss, I don't smoke, I don't drink, and I read the bible daily."

Soon thereafter I had another elderly patient 104 years old. So I asked him the same question, "What do you attribute your long live too? He told me the following; "I smoke, I drink, I cuss, and I chase the women." This was a very interesting dichotomy between the two patients.

In actuality your life expectancy depends upon several factors, but mostly the genes your parents pass on to you have the greatest influence. You could have great longevity genes passed on but you participate in race car driving. You now have the added risk of crashing regardless of your genes.

Then there are some people who have both the gift of health and financial security. My amazing uncle is one of those fortunate people. As of this writing my uncle is 98 years old and sharp as a whip. He walks faster and probably thought faster than I do. My amazing uncle is on top of all current events and could debate with the best of them. He is so passionate about his opinions.

His memory is as sharp and acute as anyone else I have seen. My wonderful uncle certainly is enjoying the Golden years. Quite frankly I wish some of his genes could be transferred to me. My uncle is living each day to its fullest. My amazing uncle worked very hard at attaining his success. Even though he is retired he still demonstrates a passion for life with zeal and zest towards every endeavor he encounters.

Faith, Confidence & Belief divided by Enthusiasm times Action equals Results, is most prominent in my uncle. You better stay on your toes and be ready for a good debate when you visit with my uncle. How refreshing it is when I visit with him. The conversations are certainly not the ordinary. Dear Uncle I dedicate the "E" of my formula to you. You certainly display its properties to the fullest. Of course great genes help but so does one's attitude and perception toward this merry-go-round called life.

My wonderful, amazing, uncle teaches us a valuable lesson. I believe my uncle would exemplify his zeal and zest regardless of his health or financial security. I believe my uncle would be successful at anything that comes his way good or bad. The question then arises, is it possible to maintain a zeal/zest towards this merry-go-round of life when it keeps throwing curve balls and repeated obstacles. Your first impression would be that character trait is unique to certain people. In a way yes, but again is it possible to choose a different perception towards life's obstacles? In other words, can we adapt to situations even though our root character traits are different. In physical therapy we use a term called plasticity. My understanding of this term is a patient's ability to adapt to the trauma they currently face.

If a person has been told his/her whole life that he/she will essentially become nothing short of a loser then what do you expect the outcome will be, and what type of personality traits will this individual take with him/her as he/she approaches the Golden years. If in your whole life that little voice inside your head says "loser you can't do that; you won't succeed; give up even before you try; it won't happen; you are no good at that etc, etc., it is not hard to predict what type of person you will be and certainly what type of person you will be in your senior years. This is regardless of having the assets called health and financial achievements. This poor person does not stand a chance of ever succeeding in the middle years or the Golden years. This person has programmed himself/herself to fail with or without even trying.

I use a famous quote from the Book "Think and Grow Rich" by Napoleon Hill circa 1920. Hill says "What the mind of man can conceive and believe he will achieve." I have seen many patients pull themselves up by their bootstraps and succeed, even though they were told by very highly trained professionals that it was not possible. As I have previously mentioned, my uncle would be successful at anything he attempted to do. Can a senior citizen have a chance of succeeding if he/she has been telling himself/herself for several years I can not do this or that?

I often hear seniors say, "The Doctor said I will never walk again or gain some physiological function." I have observed that those seniors, in spite of their medical problems, accomplish feats that will give you goose bumps and make the hair on the back of your head stand up.

The Golden years are not so Golden when your health, your financial security, your loved ones, and you memory is gone. Is it possible to enjoy your Golden years with these factors? What do you think the answer is? I hope when you finish reading this book and re-read it then you can come to an answer.

Let us continue the adventure with more food for thought.

The Triangle of Life

I have frequently used a diagram that I call the triangle of life throughout this book. In my viewpoint life is composed of the physical elements, the emotional elements and the spiritual elements. The physical aspect is in the lower left corner, the emotional aspect is located in the right corner and the spiritual aspect is at the top. We are striving to achieve a balance between all three although I have given examples that at different times in our lives each aspect may be getting more of our attention than other aspects.

Explore each aspect with viewpoints and examples. The physical aspect encompasses the physiology of human workings. In other words how we work falls into this category my organs; how my heart is doing; my liver; my lungs, and all my other anatomical parts. This aspect of our existence gets most of our attention on a day to day basis. In fact so often I have seen chronic diseases become so predominant that a person's specific characteristics gets lost and become the disease instead of maintaining their own uniqueness/qualities that they bring to this world. They become the disease. As one approaches the Golden years and are dominated by a chronic disease it keeps telling them you can not get better. "We are doing our best."

How is it possible for these individuals to even entertain the idea of enjoying the Golden years? I propose the question; Is it possible to (1) to change ones attitudes, perceptions, opinions, (2) overcome the devastating effects of chronic diseases, constant internal verbiage saying it is not possible, you are what you are, (3) it is not possible to change at all. Do these individuals even have a chance ?

The emotional aspect encompasses how one deals with the psychological events that are constantly presenting themselves. How do you react to the infamous word "stress"? Stress has such a strong influence on how you interact with this merry-go-round called life. Emotional balance is constantly varying from (a) feeling good about yourself and the world around you, (b) depressed with an ongoing feeling that things are not going to get any better, hopelessness and helplessness that this is the best it will be.

Thank God we have professionals who are highly trained to help, mentors who seem to come into our lives when we feel our worst; parents who give of themselves to see that our lives are a little better than their lives were; religious leaders who come down off the pulpit with words of compassion and support in times of need; friends who are always there to offer a shoulder to lean on, and of course spouses/significant others who choose to share their lives in good and bad times. Lastly, the greatest support we could ever imagine comes from our God.

The spiritual aspect which sits on top of the physical and emotional has been defined for thousands and thousands of years. The definition itself is opened to countless variations of interpretations. Suffice it to say that my interpretation is that aspect of oneself that is the image of God. That holy gift of God's image is impressed upon our existence. That spark of life is connected directly to God. That aspect of our existence does not return to earth the time of our death. That aspect returns to God even though it appears that the spiritual aspect is subdued in our body where the emotional, mental, and the physical components dominate.

The top of the triangle is the spiritual aspect. Think of a triangle in three dimensions (a pyramid). All points of this three dimensional triangle lead to the top. How one gets to the top is so varied that the choice is literally an individual approach? Does one take a direct approach or does one go a little to the right, then a little to the left or even downward? It is your free will to choose how you will get too the top. Never forget you will eventually get to the top. In fact, again in my opinion, the road trip begins at the beginning of life. What a gift from the creator. You get to choose the route, and you get to change your mind. You get to experience the adventure, good or bad, right or wrong, moral or immoral, ethical or not ethical. The journey leads to the top.

There are people whose lives are less tumultuous than others. In fact during a person's life he/she will probably experience both smooth and rough waters. There are people whose lives experience nothing but rough waters. In spite of the consistency of the water the road leads to the top, with you (the captain) steering/choosing the path you want. This is the gift of God to his children, the free will to choose at any point in your lives what path to take regardless of genes, life's experiences, youth or senior, rich or poor, educated or not educated.

Is it possible to change in spite of physical components, emotional aspects or constant verbiage telling us you can not do something? Did Helen Keller choose to change by accepting her teacher Ann Sullivan. What was the outcome? Helen Keller was one of our great women of the 20th century. Did Thomas Edison choose to continue experimenting with the development of the electric light bulb to the extent of over 10,000 experiments that failed, or as Edison said, "I ran out of experiments that were failing."

Did my grandfather choose to come to America to better himself and his family
before Hitler started his genocide of Jews, Armenians, and all others who had imperfections according to that lunatic? My grandfather

did not speak the English language, had no money or special skills, but he had a passion, an enthusiastic, attitude, and perseverance that he would succeed. My grandfather built a very successful business gathering remnants and recycling it back to the manufacturers. He repackaged rags. My grandfather was so successful he was able to buy a building in downtown Manhattan (New York City). My grandfather was so successful he brought many of our relatives to this country and started them off on their road to the American dream.

Did Franklin Roosevelt choose to run for office even though he was handicapped with polio? Did he become one of our greatest presidents? Did he have the belief this country can come out of the depression, and battle the tyranny of Hitler and the emperor of Japan? Did he not give a speech that changed the course of our nation, "You have nothing to fear but fear itself?" Did our nation see as a unified people that our president was correct? Did we not come together as one and turn back tyranny?

Did not our parents' generation build a nation into a super powerful nation? Did we not choose as a melting pot of various peoples to give to less fortunate people throughout the world, in spite of being disliked by so many. Look at your dollar bill. On that dollar bill is printed, "In God We Trust" we are one nation under God... All roads lead to that aspect called spirituality. Did not our founding fathers and of course the pilgrims come to this land to experience religious freedom. To sit down and even write my opinions without the fear that I will be jailed or put to death for my particular opinions, is a testimony to a free nationality is so obvious that free will and choices one makes will eventually lead to the top. I can choose my interpretations of the Golden years. Again, I ask you if you can change?

Aging & the Triangle of Life

Aging is the process of becoming.

Definition: "The whole duration of a person or thing since birth or beginning. That part of the duration of a being which is between the beginning and any given time. A certain period of human life, as infancy, youth, manhood and old age." For the purpose of this book aging is the process of getting older. We used the term the "Golden Years" to signify the older part of our existence. We have emphasized the senior years and have used seniors to demonstrate what is so good about aging (getting older).

I used the example of a triangle where the physical aspect and the emotional aspect are located at the lower corners. The pinnacle of the triangle is our spirituality. I have defined each aspect as it relates to the aging process. In actuality the aging process begins when life begins. As I have mentioned in reference to cell physiology we reach a so-called balance at around 21 years. To clarify this point I do not mean men mature earlier or are more mature than woman. What is meant here is overall there are cumulatively more cells dying than being created at around 21 years old for men, and around 25 years old for women. What is so good about aging? From the physical aspect the body wears out with time. When you are hurting is that a good thing? Do you feel good about hurting? Pain is an interesting stimuli in the human body. You can remember the pain but the actual hurt (from a physical perspective) is not there.

When a woman gives birth, that is real pain. Twenty years later that mother can remember in great detail the episode of giving birth and how hard it was pushing a small baby approximately the size of a bowling ball through a small opening. That memory of pain can bring back that birth day but the actual hurt is probably forgotten. In other words the brain will remember the pain, but not the hurt unless the pain nerves are stimulated. The interesting thing about pain is it has to be stimulated (the nerve endings specifically for pain) for the brain to feel the hurt, in spite of the memory of the pain. Chronic pain is where the nerve endings are constantly being stimulated and the messages are reaching the brain. So, you hurt until those nerve endings are quieted.

In the physical realm can one say anything good about pain, at any age. I guess the only thing that comes to my mind is the hope that the doctors will prescribe medicine, or some other technique to stop the receptors. Can you say anything good about the pain itself? Here's one idea to ponder. Without pain the body would have a difficult time surviving in this environment. You need pain as a warning signal that something is not right like a warning light on your car. The car will continue to run but if you ignore the temperature warning light the car will probably overheat. If your body gives you a warning signal and you ignore it then there might be danger to your body awaiting you. If you sprain/strain your ankle and there are no pain signals then further danger to that joint might ensue. The pain will stop you in your tracks so you will have to deal with the injured ankle. The problem arises when these receptors do not shut off and a chronic state follows. A condition called fibromyalgia demonstrates this quite clearly. The pain receptors do not shut off. So I asked my patient who happens to have this affliction, can you say anything good about your predicament? What is so good about the aging process when you are inflicted with fibromyalgia? Here is the dilemma you really can't survive without the sensation of pain but when it doesn't shut off there's nothing good about it.

Now this chronic pain pattern will eventually affect the mental/emotional realm. Can you imagine having a nerve ending called pain never shutting off? Day in and day out, night/day, you are constantly hurting. How is it possible for an individual to say anything good about the aging process? The mental perception changes from an individual full of vim and vinegar, anticipating the next day to a condition in which one does not look forward to another day of the same hurting. It is enough to drive one crazy. Can you imagine walking up to someone who is in this situation of chronic pain and you are not? "Now come on Mrs. Smith, life will get better, hang in there, let us work towards these goals. If that person doesn't throw you out of their room I would be surprised. You have to match their tone. I am not saying have their pain, but be empathetic towards their plight. I have used that approach of being empathetic, emphasizing the small gains and focusing on achievements. I find this works best for my particular approach to healing.

Over the years I have seen numerous patients decrease the pain and return to having vitality and zest for life. Regaining physical attributes follows right behind. From that perspective, the challenge of accomplishing those outcomes lies in the realm of possibilities. Remember that word, "possibilities," because that is a potent word in the "what is so good about aging" theme of this book. You would think that a person's tolerance for pain either acute, or chronic would increase with age. That is a toss up. As an athlete I endured pain - playing with bruises, and broken bones. Being in the heat of the game I did not give it much of my attention. The next play was more important. I was able to distract my focus of attention to something else. Now here is another fact about pain. Your brain will only interpret the highest stimuli to reach those receptors and make you hurt. For example; you are suffering from a bruised finger, but unfortunately you just dropped a heavy object on your right big toe. The toe pain is far greater in intensity than the thumb. Your focus of attention is now to the toe, in spite of the thumb pain. Or you take pain medicine that completely blocks the receptor sight in your brain. The brain does not interpret the pain signal at all, even though the distant receptor is firing signals to the brain. In fact you have chemicals in your body that duplicate this reaction like a pain medicine called endorphins. The key is how to stimulate these endorphins to be released? We are researching this topic and coming up with new information everyday. It is not good that you are suffering, but it is good to be alive so you can learn how to do this. That is the potential/possibility. Many individuals are doing it on a daily basis through the help of various highly trained professionals.

What's so good about this pain scenario and aging? As one grows older and is exposed to new stimuli the brain makes synapses to handle this information. Essentially an older person has the possibility of having more synaptic capacity than a younger person. A potential exists to develop new pathways of learning. Here is the "Oh Yeah" the brain cells are dying off faster than when we were younger. In spite of this dichotomy I have seen this potential manifest itself and people improve their function. In a way it is a miracle but also a fact of human physiology given to us by God, a little different way of looking at the same picture. This kind of makes you think outside of the box.

From the emotional aspect you have been given the gift of thought. Within this thought is a concept called attention. In the waking state you can choose where and what you focus your attention on. As previously explained, if you change your attention from one sensory receptor to another your brain will interpret the most intense one. You do have the potential within you. That brain program comes with Windows XP manufactured by God.

Another very valuable tool within this program is your ability to imagine. To summarize, we have several tools at our disposal, i.e., focus of attention, the possibility to change, your imagination, and thought just to name a few. You can be taught to use these tools no matter what age you are. What is needed are the FCB divided by E times A to get the results. To understand that their exists the possibility it can occur. NEVER, NEVER, give up the hope that it can occur. You never know, when some young brilliant student is on the threshold of Discovery with some new technique, medicine, or some way of bringing those endorphins out.

Look at all the new medical discoveries in the past 40 years. It is possible and don't give up the hope that it is always a potential possibility that a new way will come to fruition. It is possible, as John F Kennedy said in the early 1960's, "By the end of this decade we will put a man on the moon and return him safely to earth." This occurred at a time when we did not even have a rocket to lift them off.

Now at the top of this triangle lies the spirituality. It is my opinion that the "image of God is here." Both roads of this triangle lead to the top. If the image of God is here, than His omnipotent, omnipresence, omni essence is here as well. The absolute pure perfection of God's creation is here. It is here that I believe no pain, no hurt, no problems exist. The innocence of pure love, compassion sharing and caring await our focus of attention. Wouldn't it be wonderful if this part of the triangle was in charge? This is what I believe the aging process affords us, the opportunity to do exactly that. I would most definitely consider that very good. The challenge awaits our discovery.

The Power of Words

It has been often said that words are powerful. Words are how we communicate. Words can bring on joy or sadness. Words inspire us and they may depress us. Words can bring on life or death. Words can be interpreted differently from one person to another. It is these differences that can bring on all of above. Words and the power they possess are only viable if we give them life itself. If we empower these words they take on a meaning defining us and guiding us. Our country is defined by documents that are housed in the National Archives called the "Declaration of Independence." The "Bill of Rights" gives us parameters which define life in this great country. However, our founding fathers set up the three divisions of government to interpret them and defend them. The words in the scriptures define our spirituality. Those magnificent words are also interpreted by our theology leaders. God gave us "free will" to make choices that define each individual's life. How we choose is defined by words and our interpretation. The power of these words, as we perceive them guide us through this merry go round called life. Life progresses and one day we awake and we are in our senior era.

Previously we perceived life via words and their meaning to us. We settled into patterns and routines, and now the Golden years are upon us. Can we break previous patterns? Can we redefine definitions we have lived by all our lives only to find out that just maybe there are different viewpoints? For example how often I have worked with patients and they were told "you will never be able to . . . So often these individuals reached deep inside themselves to accomplish astounding achievements. The interesting thing is that this occurs regardless of age. Words like wisdom, thoughts, imagination, passion, possibilities, laughter, and philosophy are so important to seniors.

You see the physical aspect is steadily declining; the emotional is not declining as quickly but we are definitely not as sharp as we were 45 years ago. This is not completely accurate.

What about wisdom, philosophy, faith, confidence, belief and possibilities. Words are powerful tools we use to set parameters on how we live. Words in our books, scriptures, and documents have no power unless we empower them. We have to digest these words and make them ours. We empower them; we believe in them. They flow through our minds and help define who we are. We allow them to change our beliefs. We react to their meanings and observe physiological changes.

When Franklin Roosevelt inspired our nation with those 10 words, "The only thing you have to fear is fear itself" it turned our nation around and the rest is history. FDR motivated, inspired and led our nation out of a depression and won a world war. John F. Kennedy made the bold statement that by the end of the decade we will land a man on the moon and return him safely to earth. We didn't even have a rocket, or moon lander. But from those words there was a belief that we can do it, and we did. I have seen in my profession when patients believe and doctors know what they are doing then the miracles occur. So how do you interpret the Golden years? Can you be inspired at 80 and can you change a lifetime of patterns to achieve a different outcome? The answers lie within you. The possibilities and potentials are within.

Words and how you digest them are just one of several tools that can make each day of your life meaningful, interesting, and exciting. Accomplishments don't stop when you retire from the workplace; wisdom does not stop when you become older. The accumulation of all your experiences just further enhances your wisdom and overall philosophy. From this perspective the Golden years are golden and the aging process is special. In our 3 dimensional triangle all roads lead to the pinnacle called spirituality. How we get there is our uniqueness. Words are just one tool of many, used to define and guide us. Use them wisely!

How Do We Treat
Our Seniors

Our nation emphasizes youth. Of all the great nations on this planet the United States of America is relatively a young nation. Our history started only about 400 years ago with the pilgrims. Are our seniors honored, respected and treated with the dignity they have earned and deserve or are seniors considered a burden to our economy because they are no longer working?

When I was growing up in Brooklyn, New York I rarely remember nursing facilities. Our Grandparents lived downstairs. Now nursing homes are so prevalent. I often recall several of my patients being admitted to our facility and no one visiting them. Children used to live close to their parents. Now my brother lives in Florida and my sister lives in New Jersey. My grandfather left his family in Poland and came to America. In China my understanding is, that the elderly are revered. Not one senior citizen should go hungry or suffer in any way.

Now that is respect and honoring our seniors. Unfortunately that is not the Case in America. It will be interesting knowing that the largest portion of our population are the baby boomers. Will our leaders and advertisers cater to this portion of the population or continue with emphasis to the young? When you are age 20 to 30 your mortality is not given a whole lot of attention. Thinking about age 50 to 60 seems so far away let alone age 80 to 90. I have a theory that time speeds up as you get older. Remember when you were 16 years old. You couldn't wait until 17 and then you could drive. Time moved so slowly back then. Now in my late 50's it seems the years are speeding by. Listening to my senior patients they ask, "Where have the years gone? I can't believe I'm 88 years old."

Our elderly should be honored, respected, and treated as an asset rather than a burden. The reality is everyone living a normal healthy life will be an elderly resident one day. We have explored in previous chapters that the physical ages steadily declines. An elderly person cannot do the same physical activities as a younger person. But the physical is just one part of the triangle of life. Life's experiences, wisdom, and philosophy are characteristics worth categorizing as assets and not burdens. We would be a lot better off if we utilized our assets rather than letting them just sit on our shelves. We can only grow in spirit and truly be that beacon to the world.

The statue of liberty states "give me your poor, your tired, your huddled masses." Our elderly are included in that famous saying that has welcomed millions to this great country. Our elderly are a very special group of people who have earned the respect from the next generation and so on. They have earned the right to be treated in a VIP atmosphere. They are a special group in our nation, who deserve our admiration, love and compassion. Not one elderly person should be suffering AT ALL. We the generations following them will make sure of that. Look past the wrinkles, the aches, the pains, the loss of short memories and know that inside that person lies the image of God. In this image is the omnipotent, omnipresence, omni essence and love for us beyond our comprehension. Now say hello to that person, with honor, respect and gratitude for their live long contributions. They have given us the ability to live in this great nation with the freedom to continue to make choices from a free will concept given to us from God and further defined by our founding fathers and the previous generation.

Does the Mind Age?

We explored components of the triangle of life, the physical at the lower left angle, the emotional at the lower right angle, and the spiritual at the top angle. We have come to a common understanding that aging is a process of movement from beginning to end (birth, infancy, toddler, adolescent, teenage, young person, adult, middle age, senior, geriatric, elderly, old age and death). These are the stages most of us hope to go through.

The most obvious component, the physical, dominates the existence of the realms. The subcategories go through the above examples and hopefully decline at a slow, steady, rate. The reality is for most of us disease presents itself throughout our life and has an effect that seems to speed up the processes of declining and brings us to our conclusion faster than we care to have it happen. Along this particular path is at times pain, suffering, lack of function, and a disharmony in our body that helps support my profession. Too say the least, in this world there is no shortage of disease.

Homeostasis is lost and we are forced to restore function, compensate for lost function, or adapt to the lost function. Those of us in the medical field can safely say that our customer base will not disappear. As we proceed in the aging process the physical component ages and declines. This temple we call our body has such a variety of programs, that it combats this disease program on a daily basis. The ability of this healing capacity is quite intense. Guyton's textbook of physiology has about 1840 pages describing in depth how our bodies work. For the most part we operate in a balanced state for most of our lives.

Disease may pop in and out of our journey of life, but we travel along this winding road unabated. There are some who do not experience the ups and downs of disease. God has blessed those individuals. We are continually learning more about the programs in our great bodies and how they work. Information is doubling so quickly that you may find what we learn today is obsolete tomorrow. Have you ever bought a computer, only to find out that in less than five years you need a new one? The capacity to hold information on your old computer can now fit inside a portable computer with space to spare. Many scientists believe we are only using about 10% of our capacity (our brain).

Look at the new computers and what they are capable of doing. Look at life now as compared to 100 years ago. Leonardo DaVinci developed a helicopter several centuries ago. Those designs worked. The problems he faced with his design were: no motors to turn the blades and no fuel source to make the motor work. Look at the last century and what humans have discovered. The resources were all here awaiting some great mind to put the pieces together. Let your imagination go and create a scene in the distant future. Our science fiction authors have been telling their stories and great visions of galaxies far, far away, and federation of planets have entertained us for years. H.G Wells told us a story of how man will get to the moon. He was not far from reality. In the movie "Phenomenon" an ordinary individual starts developing more synaptic connections in his brain and miraculous events occur. He begins to use more than 10% of his brain. These fictional characters are not that far from reality. With new discoveries in medicine our lives have been enhanced.

Diseases that would have killed years ago are no longer a threat to us. Newborns that would have never made it past their first day are alive thanks to our discoveries. Inventions to make our lives easier are now common knowledge but unthinkable centuries ago. Where would the world be without "Velcro" or "Duct Tape?" Can you imagine a world without cellular phones, without the Internet, without airplanes, air conditioning, and automobiles? The physical realm is constantly changing and improvements in all aspects of this physical realm are coming to fruition.

What about the emotional(mental) component? Here again we see great strides in mental health. We have more time on our hands to seek the enjoyment of life and its interpretations. Centuries ago one had to work from dawn to dusk at least six or seven days a week. Who heard of retirement back then? Retirement meant death. Who had time to take a vacation, see a movie, or take a cruise? You worked and that was it. In comparing the great strides between the physical and emotional components it is greatly imbalanced in favor of the physical category.

This world is mostly dominated by physical components. Our triangle of life is quite imbalanced between the physical and emotional aspects.

Let's send our attention to the top of the triangle, the spiritual aspect. For centuries we humans have attempted to define and interpret God's message and guidance for us (his creations). My children bought me a book about the history of religion. It mentioned that there are over thousands different types of religions and thousands of names we call God.

A timeline gives us a perspective of religions and world cultures. For example, around 2500 B.C. Judaism was developing. However at 4000 B.C. Hinduism started. Zoroastrianism 1200 B.C., Jainism 600 B.C., Taoism 600 B.C., Buddhism 500 B.C., Confucianism 500 B.C., Christianity

A.D. 4, Islam A.D. 622 and Sikhism A.D. 1500. The point here is that Human kind is seeking out relationships with God and how to define that relationship by their particular tenets (rules/regulations-the how to practice that particular belief). The need to explore this relationship with God appears to be a deep seeded drive in us. Unfortunately humankind is still at the beginning stages in my opinion. Man is still killing man (Cain is still killing Abel his brother). We are still divided by various differences in our beliefs and relation with our God. We are still separated by color, creed, and nationality. Even though our great nation was founded on the concept that "All men are created equal" it is only if you happen to be in the majority. The exploration of our spirituality is in its infancy. In my opinion this is analogous to our aging processes. When we were in our infancy we were dependent upon our parents for survival. They told us what to eat, what to wear, where to go, and what to think. In other words their viewpoints and interpretations about life and God was what we were supposed to follow. As we age into adulthood, we leave our parents' home along with its particular rules and regulations. We begin to venture into our own opinions and viewpoints about life and God.

Constantly we are under the influence of our parents' ideas about life. Every once-in-awhile individuals come along and break the pattern. These historical individuals break the pattern and use a little more than 10% of their brain and bring to us their thoughts and ideas inspired by God. Moses took a nation of slaves and brought them out of Egypt; Jesus had the courage to stand up to the religious leaders of the day and present God's visions and teachings to humanity. Martin Luther stood up against the Catholic powers of that time to start the Protestant movement. From that we have our Baptists, Methodists, Lutherans, Pentecostals, and Unitarians. In our triangle of life there are many ways to the top. Judeo-Christian, Islam, Buddhism, Hinduism the list goes on. God inspires us all in such a unique way. The diversity is so apparent that diversity itself appears to be one of Gods many gifts to us.

An interesting side note is that of all the human beings who have ever walked on this planet. No two people have had the same fingerprint. Every single person has had his or her own unique fingerprint. This top of the triangle has been involved with presenting differences of opinions that wars have been waged over those differences. We are growing, very slowly but proceeding forward.

All Roads Lead to Your Spirituality

Well, here we are on a particular road coming out of the physical region. Our road appears to be never ending with dips, curves, and straight portions. We continue to accumulate experiences. These experiences are kept in our memory programs for future reference. It seems that this road never ends. Then when we least expect it this road connects with another road that comes from the emotional region. Again numerous experiences are accumulated and stored. We seem to be always going forward but we are unable to see an end in sight. Several rest spots along the road serve as refreshing stations. We rest here and gather our agendas and move on. Various other people seem to enter then suddenly leave our road. No one is forcing us to move forward but an underlying presence seems to be nudging us forward. Before we even realize where we have come from or where we are going we are elderly individuals. We say to our colleagues "Where did the years go?" The underlying force keeps nudging us forward always forward. Finally we are approaching the city limits for the spirituality region. The door slowly opens and we get our first peek of this region. WOW our eyes can't believe what they see. Beautiful blue skies, warm breezes, lush greens, tropical foliage, aromatic scents beyond whatever we have previously experienced. A deep sense of tranquility prevails. A sense of peace and harmony flows freely around and through us. Our sensorial is bombarded with so many stimuli, that it can't keep up with the input. We are greeted by old and new friends who have such a sense of love and enthusiasm that it just flows off of them. Sense of peace both inwardly and outwardly sing a beautiful soft tone that is pleasing to our ears. An underlying presence that is so familiar to us speaks to us without words. We understand the voice, which is so familiar to us. The calmness along with peace and quiet, is so contagious in lieu of several individuals apparently very busy with what appears to be tours. Laughter is everywhere; looking around there are several large structures like the old Greek temples.

A great peace is experienced by us all. Answers to any question we might have almost immediately are made clear to us. I noticed a large Oak tree just to my right. I walked over to it and sat down on the benches. In an instant an old friend is sitting next to me. We begin sharing our life experiences. I remember every minute detail without any effort. In another instant an old patient is conversing with me. I remember many years ago telling this patient that we would continue our conversation under a large Oak Tree. I continue to converse with thousands of old friends, relatives, and old patients. The interesting thing about this is that there is no concept of time. Just being in the moment is the feeling I get. The beauty of this place keeps intensifying. Then I hear in the distance what appears to be a phone ringing. I turn my attention to that ring and in the next moment I'm back in my bedroom where the phone is ringing. The phone stops ringing and I just sit on the edge of the bed absorbing what I have just experienced. Ever have those dreams where you wish the dream can continue? I ask myself if that is a dream or a coming attraction. It is my opinion that the spirituality region is the real thing and all of the roads I've taken from the physical region to the emotional region lead to the spiritual region. All I can say is "Thank you God for the coming attractions." I am just in awe of what my mind has experienced. I really felt like a kid in a mega toy store. My aches and pains were absent, my personal afflictions were also absent. The bounce in my step had returned. The sense of immortality was once again with me. It was like my youth had returned. My memories were crystal clear. My eyesight as well as my other 5 senses was keen. My thoughts were immediately turned into actions. I was able to fly and basically go anywhere my thoughts took me. It was true; the image of God is in the spiritual region.

I wanted to go back to that region. Then a soft kind loving voice made its message clear to my mind, "in do time my child." There was no fear just "Faith, Confidence, and Belief" in that powerful kind recognizable voice. Then the voice said, "I am that I am and I love you, welcome home." I realized at that moment I was "back" in the 57 year old body with all its accumulated afflictions and yet the sense of still being in the presence of God and all the experiences I had were still around me and through me. At first, the door to the spiritual region at first appeared very difficult to open. Once opened it pivoted open and closed with the gentle wind of a spring day. I thought to myself, did I just have a near death experience? Then a quiet voice said, "NO it is that it is." I can't begin to tell you the goose bumps and shivers up and down my spine were flowing intensely. I had just realized that my life long goal had just come to fruition. My spirituality was who I really am and my spirituality had become awake and activated. My physical and emotional regions were not dissipated but subjugated to a lower level of my existence. The little boy of my childhood was not forgotten but part of my foundation pillars help support my growth. It is that growth which has led me to opening my spirituality; it is the who of whom I really am.

With regard to the spiritual region, my answer is "no" to the question does your mind age? God created man in his image, and is alive and very real. It is this author's perception that it is located in the spirituality region, a region that so effortlessly opens its doors and all roads lead to it. It is an area of no boundaries, unlimited potential utter peace and beauty. It is truly the image of God, omnipotent, omnipresence, and omni essence - a place to call our home. I believe this to be true; it waits for us just around the corner. Love it and embrace it for it is truly who we are...

Your Assets

Assets are additions to the quality of your life. They include many different aspects, for example the assets that contribute to your physical aspects. This region is the most obvious. Your health is one of the greatest assets you have. When good health is present you enjoy life and want it to continue forever. Good health includes all of your body parts working in harmony. We call this homeostasis, a balance amongst all of the cells in your body. It is interesting that having pain or not having pain sometimes means you are healthy. For example it you are walking around and you slip on the curb your ankle might sustain a sprain/strain (an overstretching of either the muscles or ligaments supporting that structure). Needless to say in all probability there is pain. This pain is a normal, expected response. This pain will make it very difficult for you to place any weight on that ankle. This is a good thing. Your body is telling you stay off the newly injured ankle and allow your body to heal that particular injury. Even though you are very uncomfortable, your body is doing what it should do. In this respect pain is an asset. If your body did not respond with pain, it is possible that further injury would incur.

Your body responses to the common cold; you feel miserable, but your body is reacting to a virus, or bacterium in a correct way. This is an asset. If your immune system was not working, then this "cold" could extend into something more serious. Your immune life for you would be next too impossible. Your five senses are assets. In fact your body's workings are all assets. Guyton's textbook of human physiology is about 1845 pages of how your body works. All of the physiological actions are assets. Just remember when anyone of these miraculous actions do not work it is a way your body tells you something is wrong. Think about how easy it is to raise your hand to scratch the top of your head. If a stroke should occur as hard as you think you can move your hand, the hand just does not move. The complexity of just speaking is an asset taken for granted until an event occurs when speech is not possible.

If we take for granted all of our workings until they are affected we have a tremendous redundant backup system that affects our physiology and can adapt to almost any event. My profession, physical therapy, deals with this concept. The ability of the body to restore function compensates for a loss or adapts to that loss. We are constantly discovering new ways for the human body to medicine is constantly discovering new approaches to treating diseases. New medicines and new surgical approaches are making our lives better. The field of Chiropractic are also developing new techniques to assist the body in dealing with disease via the vital correlation of the nervous system and function. All the fields of alternative medicine that bring out the inner body's ability to self heal. The greatest medicine ever developed if left on the shelf and never taken into the body will do nothing. It will just sit there and sit there with and nothing will happen. The greatest Chiropractic adjustment will do nothing if the human body is not present. I am stating the obvious here, of course, but we do tend to take it all for granted. You see the greatest asset is your body and the health of it. So next time you "catch that dreaded cold" and you feel miserable, smile a little and just say thank you that your body is working correctly in fighting off that virus or bacterium.

We can stay in the physical region for all of the thousands of daily workings our body employs to keep us in balance, but let's move to the emotional/mental region. Emotion comes to my mind immediately. Let's look at the concept of laughter. Laughter affects your physiology in a most positive way. Laughter heals in fantastic almost miraculous ways. A famous editor contracted a serious disease. He was not responding to traditional approaches, in fact he was dying. This individual decided to go home and die. Well he did not just stay idle he got himself every comedy he could get his hands on. While watching these movies he laughed himself back to health. He faced his destiny, took charge, and laughed himself back to health. Perseverance is an asset to admire. Thomas Edison in developing the light bulb experimented over 10000 times before he got it right. How long would you stay at one thing before frustration sets in and you stop?

These emotions are present regardless of the age bracket you are in. Can an 85 year old learn new functional mobility tasks? In my 33 years I would say absolutely yes. In fact that is what my profession is all about. Restoring function regardless of the age. Add passion to perseverance and now you are increasing the odds of accomplishment. Add action to the equation by seeking out that individual who has the same characteristics and wow the results seem to come more quickly. Now add conviction, dedication, compassion, knowledge, and a deep clarity that the outcome will happen. You can now begin to understand why some people get the results they set their minds on and others may or may not achieve those same results. Remember previously I asked the question "are you sure the sun will rise in the east tomorrow?" I mean are you convinced that event will occur. Well I would say that the answer to that question is yes. In fact every part of me will unanimously say yes. That kind of assuredness and conviction when put into play will get you the results you requested. That clarity of determination that the task will occur helps the task to occur. Well "maybe I will get that, or maybe I will try to get that." I like the line in the movie star wars when

Yoda says "try or try not, do or do not." Don't try just do it.

Words are powerful and they imprint on your mind to get things done. When you enter a command into your computer, the computer does not *try* to do it, it just does it. Right or wrong it just does it. In other words it takes action. There are some powerful tools inside of you in all regions (physical, emotional and spiritual). All of these thousands and thousands of tools are your assets. Good or bad it is your free will (choice) to make.

As I have said earlier the spiritual region is located at the top of the triangle of life. All roads lead to this region. In my opinion, this is where the image of God is mainly located. This region appears to be second to the physical and emotional. However, this is the most potent responsive area that, in my opinion, is most directly intertwined and responsive to God If you listen to God's conversations with you. Thank you Neil Donald Walsch for you tremendous insight and courage to put into words so powerful a statement of our relationship with God. You have inspired me and thousands. Every aspect of this spiritual region is an asset.

It is here that your connection to God reveals God's awesome power and insight. God's image is here in you. The free will choices you make in your lifetime come to fruition. Omnipotent, omnipresence and omni essence are all here. The beginning and the end, the alpha and the omega, the I am that I am are all here in God's image to us his children.

Through unconditional love God's gifts are given to us. We can choose to explore the possibilities or not. We can choose to focus all of our attention in the physical region or the emotional region if we want to. We can believe anything we choose to believe. We can use our choices wisely or stupidly. Common sense is not so common. In looking at our history on this planet, we are still at the level of Cain killing Abel. We still see our fellow human beings as apart from us and in my opinion apart from God. We are still empowering others in telling us how to do this or that. God gave us a brain with infinite possibilities and we are still focusing our attention on petty things. How many toys one accumulates is given more attention than the person's characteristics. God always sends messages and leaders to guide us through life's ongoing trials and tribulations. In my field I spend a lot of time convincing patients that there exists a possibility that they may get well. The elderly are so often, through the years, convinced that they cannot accomplish this or that. Well ponder the several stories I have shared about ordinary people accomplishing extraordinary events. Your assets are endless, your possibilities are endless, your potential is endless. Your capacity to learn, share, love, accomplish, and respect are all endless.

All of these assets are the gifts of life. We explored the physical region and one just has to pick up any textbook of physiology to completely understand the complexity of the whole thing. Thousands and thousands of chemical reactions, functional tasks, millions of signals all reaching your brain. That organ that sits on top of your shoulders is always on. It is always filtering, compartmentalizing, and deciding where what and how you will react to this merry-go-round called earth.

Life's constant experiences are all kept neatly organized for you. Retrieval is almost instantly. This physical body is constantly performing one miracle after another. In fact, even when disorganization occurs (disease) the body will adapt and compensate for that particular loss. Just look at someone who has survived the polio epidemic. To this day I do not know how some of these individuals even walk. They defy the textbooks. As the expression goes they did not read the book.

The compensatory mechanisms individuals employ when born with "defects" is a miracle to observe. Having worked with these people is all inspiring. It is possible for an elderly patient to restore, compensate, and adapt themselves to their deficits regardless of what they have been told or what they have chosen to believe. The assets of passion, wisdom, excitement, laughter and philosophy are at their disposal. Many of my elderly patients are not aware of these tools that are right inside of them. You see Leonard DaVinci's helicopter did fly, only at that time no one had developed a fuel or a motor too make it work. Those resources were on earth at the time but the mind of mankind was not there to develop it at that time.

Use your imagination and explore the possibilities of where mankind can go. What can mankind accomplish, in the field of medicine, in let's say 100 years from now? I refer you to the many books available for this subject. But suffice it to say your imagination is only limited by you. What can mankind accomplish in the emotional region? This region appears to age a little slower than the physical. Passion, excitement, and laughter, should be opened when an individual chooses to open it. The accumulation of all life's experiences lends the elderly to enhance their most gifted assets...philosophy and wisdom. Those are assets we all can use regardless of age. We often say that the greatest asset our country has is its children. I would like to add that the elderly are in that category as well. What our parents and grandparents have accumulated in their philosophy and wisdom can most definitely help the next generation.

It is a loss when this asset is not used. How often we say I should have listened to my parents' advice etc.. The gift of life is the aging process and what we have experienced along the journey. How we use our experiences to make one's life balanced is the gift. The challenges facing all of us are so diverse and yet so common amongst our age groups. Do you remember the challenges you faced in high school? The most important thing was not the economy but what person you hung out with or what girl/boy you would like to date. Then going onto college, or what type of occupation you will do after high school entered into the equation as graduation approached. Now you are married and have a family. The challenge here is survival.

For some of us success happens in many aspects. We are blessed with a wonderful spouse, healthy children and an occupation that leads us to enjoying the rewards of earning a nice living. We are now aging and the children are on their own. The challenges here are health issues. Again some of us are blessed with a balanced health and are rarely sick. However, most of us will be using the health system for our particular ailments.

In the 2008 election year one of the major issues is health reform. How can we insure every American? The cost of medical care is skyrocketing and basically out of control. It is here that our elderly population appears to not be an asset but an expenditure. How sad that those individuals worked so hard to make our nation great, paid their share of taxes, and are considered an expenditure. Those individuals are our assets and nothing short of unconditional love, respect and admiration is their right. Now listening to this idea and being told either directly or indirectly they are a so called burden to society. The elderly population, if they should get sick do not stand a chance of restoring their function because they are old. This is only my viewpoint on this subject. Just imagine how their health would improve if their attitudes would be from an asset point of view. I have said throughout this book that your perception is your reality. Perceive that you are a burden to your family and society in general and you become a burden. Perceive that you cannot do this or that and guess what you can't. Perceive that you are an asset to society, and you can continue to restore, compensate, and adapt to whatever life throws at you.

I have heard comments like "Guess what, my mother hasn't walked in years. My mother has returned to her home thanks to you. I can't believe my husband is standing again. My father who had a stroke is communicating again thanks to you and your staff." These are the comments I have heard throughout my years in the medical profession. The miracles are ongoing because life is a miracle and what we possess inside of us is just plain miraculous.

We are created in God's image with essentially unlimited possibilities. The choices are ours to make in a free will parameter. You can change because we are so diverse in our physical region, emotional region and our spiritual region. Thought does manifest into matter on a daily basis. Our thoughts are inspired and connected to God. We are not apart from God but part of God. Choose your perception and enjoy the experiences good or bad. We are constantly learning about ourselves and our connection to nature. We are part of this universe. We are as important and loved by the creator in all of God's creations. Look up at the night sky. Look at all those stars. We are part of all that you see, hear and feel. The possibilities are limitless. You can do as I did, said a great individual thousands of years ago. Through me all is possible.

Possibilities

Where are we going with all these ideas, words, concepts and perceptions? Our journey continues beginning with entertaining the possibility that something exists beyond our current knowledge base. When Christopher Columbus lived the going idea was that the earth was square and if you sail west the inevitable would occur; you would just fall off the face of the earth, never to be seen again. This brave explorer, as history tells us, convinced the Queen to fund an expedition to explore a new passage to the near east and bumped into the "New World." His determination, imagination and conviction were the forces behind the scenes pushing Columbus ever so forward. The idea that the earth was flat was just silenced.

Throughout history mankind's curiosity has led him to discover new worlds, new ideas that through inspired thought came reality. It was once said that a Catholic would never be elected to the Presidency. John F Kennedy did not read the memo. We are so far behind the Russians in the space race there is no way we can win. Our young President Kennedy declared with utter confidence that we will put a man on the moon and return him safely to earth by the end of the decade (1960's). Well I guess NASA did not read the memo. Helen Keller will never see or hear again and essentially not contribute anything to society her parents were told at the time. Her teacher, Anne Sullivan, also did not read the memo. You see Helen Keller, in my opinion, was one of the greatest people of the 20th century. Even though she could not see or hear, she adapted and compensated for those losses and did see and hear just in a different way.

I had a patient who was diagnosed with terminal cancer and given a few weeks to live. This person had a deep desire to attend her class reunion. The only problem was the reunion was several months away. Well past the time she was told that was left what do you think happened? You are right; she did not read the memo. This elderly lady lived to attend her class reunion. Shortly after that she passed away. I have countless memories of patients who have initially read the memo but met me. I usually do not read or even listen to the memo. I focus my attention on the spiritual region first. Here all possibilities are just that possible. Then I focus on the emotional region. It is here where a person's perception and attitude help dictate physiological actions.

I look at the physical region. Put all three together and the possibilities are just that possible. O.K. What if an elderly patient listens to you and begins to explore the possibilities of all three regions. That person then goes back to his/her room, looks in the mirror, and the image in the mirror looks back and says, "Oh yeah."

You still have crippling arthritis, you still are not walking, or you still have the after effects of the stroke. So who are you kidding? This is absolutely correct if you read the memo. Obviously Helen Keller, Anne Sullivan, Thomas Edison, Napoleon Hill, John F Kennedy, my grandfather, your parents, Henry Ford, the Wright Brothers, Dodie, Felicia, Franklin D.

Roosevelt, and all the thousands of patients that I have had the privilege to work with did not read the memo. All those brave explorers and soldiers kept the faith and succeeded. Our founding fathers created a country under God indivisible for liberty and justice for all. Dr Martin Luther King had a vision and brought it to thousands of people black or white. The list is endless, the possibilities are endless, and you have to NOT READ THE MEMO. I can hear a skeptic saying your words are interesting but you are giving false hope to people with real afflictions. OH REALLY. Tell that to my patient who suffered a spinal cord injury and could only move small parts of his arm. We were able to enhance the functional movement and believe it or not this individual was taught how to drive a van. He was able to use the electric lift and he went cross country. HOPE is not false. Hope is that want or desire in expecting some good outcome. A desire for some good is not false, unless you read the memo. A saying that I used to have on my desk said "Expect a Miracle Today." I would like to add, "Accept a Miracle Today."

We are beginning to uncover new physiological discoveries. Medicine is doubling in its understanding of how we work almost every five years. The computer you just bought will probably be outdated in 5 years or less. The Internet is exploding across this planet in record number. Thirty years ago who even heard of the Internet? Well the visionaries did not read the memo. We are told that our natural resources, i.e. fossil fuels, are running out. Well this might just stimulate our visionaries to discover new energy sources. I am sure there is another Thomas Edison out there already working on the challenge. In this chapter on possibilities do not read the memo. Do not buy into the concept that it is not possible. You the elderly, read the words of this book over and over. Possibilities do not end with the aging process. They just begin. Oh I hear the skeptic again. But the reality is I have this disease and that disease and I can not do that anymore or I can not do this anymore. I am just waiting for God to take me. Well as I have previously said, DON'T READ THE MEMO. Do not limit yourself to anything. Yes in the physical region you are aging and systems are declining, the emotional region not as fast, but the spiritual region is just beginning to be explored. You see as we approach our mortality, we hope all those sermons we attended and were taught will come to fruition on our passing.

You see not too many people have come back to tell us what is going on. Not completely true. Several books have been written on the near death experience.

Several interpretations on the HOLY SCRIPTURES have been passed on from one generation to another. God constantly gives us insight into the entire picture. All you have to do is LISTEN. Inspiration is not just for a chosen few. It is available to everyone. Let's let our imagination fly for a few moments. What if the top of the triangle was in charge and the lower angles were secondary and tertiary respectfully? From birth we have be ingrained with this concept. Our spirituality rules our existence. It is from this region that all of our experiences, and interactions with our fellow humans occur. Spirituality dominates and directs all actions in the physical. It is not the spiritual that is encased in a physical body, but the physical and emotional body is in the spiritual region. I guess one could say heaven on earth or heaven in us. The who we really are is the spiritual region. The physical and mental regions are sub categories allowing us to participate in the physical and emotional components of life here on this physical planet. When you turn the computer on the main operating system comes on. The sub systems like the Internet, and a word processing program needs to be double clicked to come on. Those sub systems are very important to the workings of the computer, but the main operating system is the key. So coming from the spiritual region first is the main operating system and your physical and mental regions are secondary.

From this main operating system (spirituality) lies our direct connection to God. It is here that we are part of rather than apart from. What then is possible here? Are there any limitations here? Are there any constraints to our thoughts? Anything and everything is possible. You see here we are created in God's (omnipotent, omnipresence, and omni essence) image. And we are part of those magnificent creative possibilities. Imagine that to all of your 45 quadrillion cells your spirituality is its creative leader like God is our creative leader to everything in existence. So from early ages you have this understanding of whom you really are and/or whom you are part of. You are capable of achieving, creating and just having fun with the whole experience. From this perception I dare any virus, bacterium, mole or anything else that has previously brought disorganization to us, to have any hold on us, unless we choose to let it be. This includes thoughts geared to put limitations on us.

Yes, my elderly patients you are that strong even though the mirror tells you differently. Do not read the memo. Change your perception and your reality has to follow. Your wisdom will protect you and guide you. Do not ever give up HOPE. It is not hopeless, it is possible, even if it just allows you to enjoy old memories. The gift of life offers you the free will to choose the program that is right for you at any given time of your life; choose wisely and realize there is no right or wrong program for your problems just different outcomes. If you do not like the outcome, then change it. It is pure and simple "Just do it" (as Nike would say). But it sounds too simple and again the skeptic is talking. Well silly, you still have the disease and you are still lying in the bed of the nursing home old and achy. What are we going to do with this skeptic? This skeptic is reading the memos. I can choose where to put my attention of focus on. I am choosing not to listen to that skeptic and I will focus my attention on the spiritual region. I will grow in understanding and implementation while in this region. You see here God is my mentor and teacher. I most definitely believe that God knows what to do for me and through "free will" I choose God as my teacher. I choose to listen to God's advice, encouragements, and suggestions. God knows what is best for me at any given time of my journey. I am excited to see what awaits me today. I look back in the past and cherish both the good and the bad as learning experiences. I imagine and dream about the future through visionary eyes with unlimited possibilities. But I place my focus of attention on the now. I live in the present.

Thank you God for being always there.

How Do You Choose
to Participate in Life

Up to this point in our journey of the aging process and what is so good about it? We have delved into many new and old viewpoints on the aging process. We have defined, or at least set some parameters to the idea. We have introduced some different concepts. We have met some of the players (my senior citizen patients and their uniqueness). A new look at life via the triangle of life. We have analyzed how aging affects this triangle. This book is made up of words. These words are powerful and once digested can affect your life and how you decide to participate in it. We explored some of the ways on how we treat our seniors.

In the chapter "All roads lead to your spirituality" we entertained the idea of possibilities for each region; the physical, the emotional/mental and the spiritual. The components of each region are your assets. Your health appears to be one of the most important components. As we continued with our expansion of new ideas, we are asked to view these regions and one's progression to the top, "Your Spirituality." These components are your assets. God's gift of life to you along with free will to choose how, what, where and why, are all assets. Which leads us to this chapter called How do you (senior citizen) choose to participate in life itself? This question probably doesn't even get your consideration until you enter the realm of senior citizen. I guess when you are eligible to join AARP you have entered this category. Prior to this date your life is speeding by with one experience after another. You barely have time to stop and smell the roses. Life is speeding by so quickly that all of a sudden you are 50 years old. What you are probably saying to yourself is "I can't believe I'm in my 50's, where did those previous 50 years go? For most of us entering the senior citizen category, we are probably still working a full time job. Our children are off on their own and for some of us, we become grandparents. Stopping to smell the roses is not in our horizon, unless a disease stops us in our tracks. Our choices are varied but who has time to contemplate roses or anything else. We are too busy making money and preparing for retirement. The aging processes are showing themselves with regularity. Our mortality is discussed, but at this period of our lives we haven't given much attention to our mortality. Having worked with the senior population for the last 20 years "death and dying" has been a common occurrence.

I have witnessed individuals facing their mortality with laughter, defeatism, gratitude and fear. So often many elderly are bitter, angry and disappointed with their lives. Many do not view their elderly years as a blessing let alone a gift. Frustration, and anger prevails for many of them. Negative attitudes dominate for most any situation. The good old days become more alive as the present stinks and future just appears to be more of the same. Their financial nest egg is dwindling quickly due to medical bills. Their spouse and close friends are gone, and their children are engrossed with the day to day operations of their families. Many of these individuals are depressed, frustrated and angry. When you first meet them in their rooms you had better match their tone or they will kick you out of their rooms.

I often observe a new therapist (young) talk down too these people and draw first impressions (judgment values) without even getting to know them. These people are very lonely and it behooves you to take a few minutes and just listen to their stories. You will be amazed at the diversity of stories, some linked directly to history. Match their tones before you start jumping into the plan of care. Ten minutes is not going to hurt the case but enhance it. When two or more are gathered in my name mountains will move and things will happen. The question is then asked how are you choosing to participate in life. Are you a character actor, an understudy. . . Are you the star, leading man/woman? Are you the director or producer? Are you a leader or a follower? Do you challenge old beliefs or just continue with the status quo? Do you grasp life by the horns and hold on for the ride? Or do you just sit on top and let the horse go where it wants to go taking the same old trail as previous days and years. Do you awake with that sparkle in your eyes? You are ready to accept the miracle for the day. What is life going

to teach me today? Who will come into my life
to change or teach me
something new?

The excitement builds from the moment your
eyes open to welcome a new day. The adventure
continues and something new will be taught too
you. You will receive some new gift and you will
give away some gift. You can't wait for the day
to proceed. Your life is an ongoing process of
experiences from specific activities leading you
to goals, and attainments. These attainments
can be goals set, or conclusions to activities
already in motion. Either way the passion for its
workings is always present. What will I be shown
today that will help me grow in all regions; the
physical, the emotional and the spiritual or will
I choose to be a pinball in a pinball machine
just hitting one bumper and then randomly
hitting another all controlled by someone else?
Will I continue to challenge common opinions?
Will I just follow the majority or will I think
my own thoughts and come up with my own
opinions? Will I buy into the stereotyping of
being an elderly individual or will I let my hair
grow long or dye my hair purple? Will I be a
free thinker, free actor, free spirit governed by
my unique spirituality? I hold to the principle

that God endorses diversity and uniqueness. This is evidenced by the fact that no two people who have ever walked on this planet have had the same fingerprint. If God endorses diversity who am I to be judgmental that my views are the only correct ones. The gift of free will and its capacity to choose is your great asset and gift from God. I endorse the freedom to choose. You are dominated by someone else telling you how to live.

The choices are there for you to make. Change doesn't stop at 75 years, diversity, uniqueness, and ongoing curiosity towards life is always present. God gave us a brain, now use it. Just decide to do it. I am part of the "I am that I am" I should be able to have my dinners comped? Well we won't go that far. Choose excitement, passion, and love for the doing. As the expression goes, "Live life to its fullest." Life is like a good wine. You sip it and then take samples. You explore all aspects of life. Let your taste buds come alive with the tools we have discussed compassion, excitement, passion, wisdom, and laugh at life itself. God invented comedy and he created mankind. What a Joke. Human behavior is quite funny and not always to be taken too seriously. The opportunities are so diverse. The road traveled is lined with several programs made to enhance your life. The door to spirituality is not as hard to open as one might think. It is much easier to open it through the eyes of a child.

Life is like walking into FAO Schwarts' toy store on fifth avenue in New York. Keep those eyes like a child. Be dazzled by the diversity of it all. Hold it forever a short time, because before you know it you are exiting this dimension and opening the door to the next adventure regardless of your beliefs. All roads lead to the top. One way is no better than any other, just a different way not necessarily a better way. Do not read the memos, write your own memos and allow the almighty to guide you and mentor you as you run through this life. Participate in it, make a difference. Turn around and help someone else like God helps you. There is hope and endless possibilities. Love it and tomorrow accept the miracle.

How Does One Open
the Region of Spirituality

As I have previously said all roads of the triangle of life leads to the top. The spiritual region is where, in this writers opinion, the image of God is mainly present. This is not to say that the image of God is not throughout every cell in your body and every emotion. You are made up of the physical and emotional. But who you really are lies in the spiritual region.

While you are a living breathing organism obeying the laws of physics and nature you are completely defined as a physical entity. At the end of your adventure here on earth your physical body is either buried or cremated.

The chemicals that make your physical are returned to earth. There is a finale to your physical entity. If you are totally defined as just a physical entity then it would end at this junction. I previously mentioned that the road out of the physical region connects with the road out of the emotional region and travels towards the spiritual region. Yes, who you are is defined in part from components of the physical and emotional regions. But these regions have a finale to their properties. You enter the spiritual region through what appears to be immovable doors. Throughout our history our sacred writings have been passed down from one generation to another. Insights into how to enter this region have be written, or spoken as myths stories or legends, from one generation to another. I will now share my insights into this discussion. I said, "All roads lead to the spiritual region and it is here that who you really are is defined." Yes the physical and emotional images are with you, but your direct link to God and his image to us, God's children are revealed. Since this region is part of whom you are along with the physical and emotional region. Then this program has to be operational from the onset of your conception. What we have is the major focus of your attention not on the spiritual region but the physical and emotional region. These two regions are the dominate ones, for the most part, while you are "alive." There is no balance between the three regions for most of one's life. Your spirituality does not become dominate until you start getting closer to your mortality. Then you hope all those biblical accounts are true. You lean heavily on your faith. This accounts for your focus of attention when you are a senior citizen.

What lies ahead for me? I am not going to discuss any particular belief/religion in this book. It is my understanding that they all offer the believer of them what they need at that time in their lives. For the most part I respect them all. The spiritual region is always open. Then the question should be asked, how do I make the spiritual region my home page? How do I live in this physical emotional body with distinct parameters and let the spiritual region be dominant? So the analogy of life's triangle should not necessarily be a triangle but two triangles put together at their bases. Then the image would be starting out with life gifted to you. This point is on the bottom. Then two lines spread out to their respective angles. On the left is the physical, and on the right is the emotional.

Then two lines emerge from these points and travel upwards to the top your spiritual region. The spiritual region is then on the bottom of the inverted triangle and at the top of the up-righted triangle. You are a spiritual entity that utilizes the physical and emotional regions to voyage throughout this planet. So again, how do we enhance the spiritual region. I believe to accomplish this feat you have to let go of all those memos that have been telling you how to think and what to believe. What courage it must have taken to face the Pharaoh and tell him "Let my people go." Only with the almighty behind you could you fathom the idea of ever approaching the pharaoh. How courageous it must have been for Martin Luther to disapprove of the tenets of the Catholic church and come up with a Protestant agenda that was different than mainstream thought at that time. The Pilgrims left their homes and traveled to the world where the dream of freedom to practice your own particular religion is possible. Then, of course, a young man named Jesus stood up to the religious leaders and preached a GOSBLE that has spread around the globe. How courageous for you and me to even think and come to our own conclusions using God's gift of free will in spite of not necessarily going with the most popular viewpoints of the day. How courageous it is for you to stand up and voice a different interpretation to common viewpoints.

It appears to me that God most definitely endorses diversity. Just look around and observe. Since no two people have ever had the same fingerprint God allows diversity. Then who are you to tell me otherwise? One of the clues these old words have said about this subject is that the way into heaven is through the eyes of a child. What does this mean? Does it mean that if I am an old person I do not stand a chance? I don't think so. Look at it from this perspective. The eyes of a child are curious, excited, twinkling, imaginative, loving unconditionally, laughter, compassionate, trusting, and innocent. This doesn't mean that if you are old age wise you cannot have those attributes. Quite the contrary, you have the choice on how you view this world and your particular voyage through it. Do your eyes (young or old) see all the possibilities this planet can do? Do your eyes gleam with passion and excitement that a new day brings? Do your eyes expect and accept a miracle at least once a day. Or do you see just an old person with pains in their joints from arthritis. You have the free will to interpret the signals that are sent to your brain for interpretation. You choose how to interpret these messages. You wanted passion then you got it. You wanted excitement then you got that. Let your imagination fly freely to whatever you so decide. One way to make the spiritual region your home page is through the eyes of a child.

Through your faith is another way to accomplish this feat. The wonderful thing about faith is that you don't have to empirically prove it. You just have to believe it. Your faith in your belief is a personal relationship between you and God. From this comes your confidence in its existence. I have always found the following to be so powerful "Be still and know that I am." The subtle power that evokes is absolutely impressive. Let us not forget the excitement you have in awaiting the results. Now the door to the spiritual region does not appear to be too hard to open.

The skeptics inside are now beginning to speak. It says, well that is all well and good but the proof is that you are old, you do have severe aches and pains and your body just is not the same as when you were 25 years old. The skeptic is right, You can't argue with that statement. Don't even try to argue that point. I repeat faith and belief in that faith does not have to be proven empirically. Again your belief is a personal relationship. It is like the skeptic saying, "Prove God exists." Well if you use your eyes to see, your ears to hear and your mind to observe the workings of us and this planet the only conclusion you can come to is that something put this whole thing together. Something is creating the molecules. Something is creating the electrons to orbit around the atom, and the stars orbiting around the universe.

What created the first energy that supposedly gave way to the so called big bang theory? Energy is not destroyed just transferred from one to another. Again where did the first energy come from? An imagination will help you enter this region. In summary you are already in the spiritual region but to make it your home page having the eyes of a child, the imagination of a visionary, the belief in your faith, and deep conviction (like knowing with all your heart that the sun will rise in the east tomorrow), possessing a deep love and respect for the creator and the creator's creations, and lastly the ability to laugh and have fun with these creations will in my opinion make the spiritual region your home page. These traits are most possible for anyone to embrace regardless of how old they are, or what state of health they are in, or what particular faith they practice. BE STILL AND KNOW THAT I AM.

Wisdom

In our continuing journey of *What is So Good About Aging*? one asset comes to mind. As we journey through life we experience various situations, and various individuals come and go. We interact with these adventures and accumulate those experiences in our memory. We are constantly adapting to the environment and making subtle changes as we journey along. Some of us have a smoother ride than others. We call those individuals lucky. For the rest of us we hit the bumps, the potholes, and even get off the road for a time and in our physical journey, we pray. Our journey is not always a smooth one. As a species we seem to adjust to most situations that come our way. Our emotional journey is a curious one. As we constantly adjust to life's merry go round our emotions experience the gamut of ups and downs, good and bad, happy and sad, at peace or disharmony. Under this umbrella of emotional and physical experiences is our free will on how we perceive those events. Based on the experiences we accumulate wisdom. And as we continue to age and experience this wisdom it intensifies. For the most part we hope that is what happens. Although when directly involved in the event it appears that we are not wiser, but just repeating the same old actions. We sit in our home now in our senior years. There is a quiet atmosphere surrounding us. Our children are on their own; our loved one has passed on and we are essentially all alone. We reflect upon all the previous years and the memories do not come forth with such clarity as they did 10 years ago. Where have all the years gone? It is at this point that one of the top emotions descends upon us. We become sad, lonely and probably depressed. Aren't these years supposed to be the "Golden Years"? This probably occurs to many of our seniors, more than reported. This is a wonderful environment for those viruses and bacterium to colonize within.

One side effect of the sadness, loneliness and depression is that our immune system is affected. STOP READING THE MEMOS. Let's perceive a different scenario. We do have free will and the ability to bring up any memory we choose, and we most definitely have the choice on how to perceive it. I have said earlier that perception is ones reality; change your perception and your reality follows. So here we sit in our home. A sense of quietness fills the home. Our physical component is having to deal with declining functions; our emotional component is having its issues, BUT, the spiritual component is flowing with love, compassion power, calmness, and joy. We know, with all our conviction that the image of God is within. In fact all of our experiences enhance the conviction that we are part of God.

There is no doubt of whom we are, why we are, how we are, and where we are. We are not alone but connected to the omnipotent, omnipresence, and omni essence, of all that is and all that will ever be. We are bathed and surrounded by unconditional love. The quiet sense of unlimited possibilities and unlimited potential is within us. The spiritual aspect is with us at creation of us. We have focused our attention on the spiritual and sub focused our attention on the physical and emotional. Remember the example of the two triangles connected. We start with the spiritual region at the bottom and from here two lines reach upwards called the physical region on the left and the emotional region on the right. From these two points the lines lead to the spiritual region again. Throughout our lives this spiritual region has been in charged. We first come from the spiritual region. It then guides us through the physical and emotional regions. We accumulate experiences, which leads to wisdom and knowledge. We get wiser and more confident of who we are and our direct connection to the almighty. The unlimited possibilities and potential to grow never stops. Individuals come into our lives and leave but share their experiences with us. We are not alone, NEVER, we are always in the presence of the almighty.

Now look at the two scenarios and choose which one you want to follow. The choice is yours. Remember nothing is impossible; change is an ongoing event. You don't like where you are then simply create a different scenario. God's gift of free will has to be the most potent action a loving creator can give us. There are no skeptics here. You know within all the cells of your body that in God's image we are. There is only quiet unconditional love within the image of the creator himself. Be still and know that I am. Listen with full focus of your attention to that voice of the creator himself. From this space you sit in your home and smile.

This wisdom just keeps growing with the aging process. You become a wiser individual and NOT an expenditure to a younger generation but an asset to all. Your accumulated knowledge of those experiences can be passed down to the next generation. I find it most interesting that in my 33 years of practice I have accumulated a vast array of knowledge on how to help my patients. It has taken me 33 years to get too that point. Yet when we hire a new graduate, they are willing to learn from an older clinician. It is possible to teach them some of the techniques that have taken me all those years? I observe the greatest compliment they can pay me, by their practice of those techniques I've shown them.

Duplicating is one of the greatest forms of flattery. And they have learned it in a much shorter period of time. We call this learning an ongoing process of experiences and accumulation of knowledge WISDOM and the application of that knowledge. As I get older in my profession I get wiser. But it is my choice to teach and pass on this knowledge to the next generation. From this perception we who are aging as a group present ourselves not as an expenditure but as assets yet to be tapped. The potential is there. As the expression goes "Use it or lose it." It would behoove the next generation to utilize us seniors for our wisdom.

I should have listened to my parents, because you know something they were right. Their advice could have saved me a lot of grief. How often do we say that to ourselves? Let's put our focus of attention on our wisdom and use it wisely. As Webster's dictionary defines it; showing good judgment; having the power of discerning and judging correctly or of discriminating between what is true and what is false, between what is proper and what is improper. Isn't that the truth? Respect and honor our elderly, they have a lot to offer and share with the next generation. Knowledge is power and our elderly have accumulated a lot of it. We are a powerful group regardless of the physical deterioration you initially see. We are, most definitely an asset to society; a group that potentially can contribute tremendously to our society.

Trust

Do you trust the scientific fact that you will age and eventually die? Of course you do. Do you trust the fact that in order to live in this country you must pay taxes? Do you trust our scientific leaders when they tell you its flu season and you need to get your flu shot in order to bypass the anguish of getting the flu? Do you trust what they say about the geriatric group as a whole? Do you trust the idea that even though the "Baby Boomers" make up the largest segment of our population the young generation rules? This is evidenced by the advertising agencies and the general attitude towards the elderly. I have never seen such emotional outbursts when the subject of skilled nursing homes comes up. "Please Mary, promise me you will never put me in a nursing home." "I will never put my mother in a nursing home." Nursing homes are disgusting and I would not put my worst enemy in one. Do you trust any of these "Memos"? I will trust you to a point, and then I am skeptical. Have you ever trusted someone or something unconditionally? To trust just for the simple sake of trusting that individual or thing; you just knew. Well if aging is an accumulation of events and you collect these events over the years then you are supposedly becoming wiser. Your confidence is growing. You rely on integrity, justice, friendship or something received in confidence. Do you trust yourself? Do you have the deep, clear trust regarding your physical attributes, emotional integrity, and of course your faith in a particular way to love and honor God. Now as you age you supposedly get wiser.

Should we trust you? I mean you are not working anymore, your health is deteriorating and you are not contributing to the country's economy. This and many other viewpoints on the elderly help segregate them from mainstream day to day operations. Since we don't trust these elderly individuals, contempt and distrust ensues. The generation that built this nation into a superpower, survived a depression, won a world war, confronted communism, is distrusted, disrespected, mocked, uncared for and too old too participate in the day to day workings of our society. What that generation forgot, we the next generation, do not even have a clue. We treat our senior citizens like an expenditure. I observe the disgust on the faces of my patients' families for having to put their parents into a skilled nursing facility. I would venture to say that loyalty is not bestowed on our elderly. What could they know, they are ancient. A note of caution, do not be fooled by just the physical. Life's experiences have made that generation quite strong and confident in their knowledge in spite of a lack of physical powers.

Having no trust in our elderly is a wrong road to travel. I do observe that the younger members of Grandma's family when they visit, look around for an escape and a very quick exit. Maybe they are facing their mortality. And this is made very clear when they visit. It is a fact of life we will age and we will die. When this lack of honor and respect towards our elderly filters down the senior's central core responds like this. The answer to who am I is usually answered like this, "I am just an old person alone not part of my kid's life because they are so busy raising their own children. My body is old and mind is tired. Dear God please take me because I am worthless. And that is a typical elderly's perception of who they are. Even though the spiritual region is so busy at the senior level, it appears ever so difficult to swim in it. The trust obviously is just not there. We are too old to make any sound decisions about anything. And the senior population buys all those memo's. The small voice inside your head is saying "SEE, I TOLD YOU SO." *Then again we ask God to take us NOW. Obviously God is in the creating business and not the destructing one. God's greatest gift is life itself.

We are endowed with numerous gifts. These gifts allow us to survive and prosper in this crazy world. Our words spoken outwardly and inwardly constantly repeat their messages. You are decrepit and sickly. I can't trust your judgment let alone your decision making capacity. I just don't trust you. And our internal voice reverberates with a loathing sound. "Who is that arrogant kid judging me in my house?" We can't help in reading the memos and buying all the gobble goop garbage. Trust is having confidence, that the correct decision will be made and having integrity to their word being fulfilled - custody over the treasures and plenty of faith, confidence and belief in their ability to make the correct decisions. Yet the older person buys into this garbage. To those skeptics I say OH REALLY. No other generation has had to raise their children and their children's children. Statistically speaking more and more children are returning home where the grandparents were kind of forced to take on this obligation.

How can we expect our older generation to participate in life when life's little nuances aren't geared to them such as narrow doorways that do not to allow a wheelchair to go through. The number of people placed in nursing homes are growing each year. More seniors have to go back to work just to pay the bills. Older people are going hungry in our country. This is outrageous! We as a nation treat our elderly dishonorable. Not one single senior citizen should go hungry or want for anything. That great generation took our nation out of a depression, through WWII, Korean war, Vietnam war several little wars. They have built this nation into one heck of a superpower. They have earned our trust, gratitude, honor, respect and our love for a job well done. How a nation treats their elderly is a commentary on the heart and spirit of that country. We have not even scratched the surface of the possibilities this generation can offer the next one. They may not be as strong, or as fast as the previous generation.

As I tell my patients when they are learning to walk and those feet just do not move as fast - remember the story of the turtle and the rabbit. Who won the race and why? When two or more are gathered in my name mountains can be moved. Let's add when two or more are gathered with trust, confidence and love then not only can mountains be moved but cities created, disease conquered, and relationships fulfilling and long. The quality of our planet would obviously intensify. Greater success in any field would simply just be there. You see as we grow older all roads lead to the spiritual region. It is here where the image of God displays to us the omnipotent, omnipresence, and omni essence quiet power of all that is, is thought becomes reality - so powerful yet so quiet, so knowing yet so humble, and so willing to just share without renumeration. Wealthy beyond one's expectations. The spiritual region is truly a place where dreams come true.

Laughter

The ability to laugh is a tremendous asset. To express the sounds and exhibit the movement of the features and body characteristics in the expression of mirth, as the dictionary defines. Have you ever laughed so hard you cried or laughed so hard your stomach hurt? Have you ever laughed so hard your bladder gave way? I once attended a Don Rickles show. Whether you like his type of humor or not, I laughed so hard tears were coming down my face. Have you ever had the giggles? Now there is an interesting expression. It seems that everything you see causes a laughing attack. What laughter does to your physiology is also a very interesting experience. Laughter actually heals you. It seems with a happy outlook towards whatever comes your way, the immune system is fortified.

Oppositely, the sad approach depresses the immune system. A depressed immune system weakens your defenses against stress, and other organisms that are just lurking in the background awaiting the opportunity to colonize and due battle with you. The characteristics of disease includes not only the physical components but the emotional ones as well. A body working in harmony does not get ill. A body working in disharmony is susceptible to all. One of the many secrets of being in a state of health is to be in a state of balance. This body made by God has a tremendous capability to remain in a harmonic state of balance. Its creator made no junk here. The countless number of redundant systems and an immune system that is constantly adapting to 500,000 bad organisms demonstrates to me, that this machine called human is quite a powerful unit. Yet on the opposite side we observe how fragile we humans are. Change the air components ever so slightly and we are gone. We function in such a narrow balance of acid and alkalinity, oxygen, nitrogen, carbon dioxide and numerous inert gases, that a slight change here would be disastrous. The temperature of our environment also demonstrates how delicate we are to fluctuations outside a narrow range for survival.

I am always amazed that on a summer Phoenix, Arizona day, where temperatures are well in the 100's our senior citizens are wearing sweaters complaining of being cold. In a way that is kind of funny. As we get older our summer electric will go down. Let's consider that another asset of getting older. Not too many species have the ability to laugh at a joke or a situation or even themselves.

I use humor in my clinical techniques. I love making my patients smile and then maybe chuckle. But when they give out a big hardy laugh I feel really good. You see, here is this 80 plus year old person who does not want to be in a skilled nursing home. It seems that one of the myths about nursing homes is that it is God's waiting room to die. If you go to a nursing home, chances are that is it for you. Pack your bags you are heading out of here real soon. I have been told that it is a very depressing environment to be in. It is a place where people just sit in their wheelchairs and wait until its there time to check out but not if you pass the rehab room.

The sounds from that room are laughter. First of all, do you know how difficult it is to make someone laugh? Ask any comedian. Laughing is so natural that to smile takes less muscles than to frown. Yet the majority of people do not walk around with a smile on their face but a frown (an angry look). So this individual has taught their facial muscles to keep a frown on. Number two, they most definitely do not want to be in the nursing home and are very angry at their families for "putting them in this place." Number three, they are angry to the world for their dilemma (their loss of control over their lives, other people making decisions for them, perks being taken away from, being treated like a child). Now that is a tough audience! So first a little smile appears, then a little chuckle and then a full blown expulsion of a funny sound call laughter.

To make these people laugh is a most challenging event. I employ this expression all the time. I kind of consider myself a stand up comic, who is keeping his day job. It seems to me that when the expression of laughter pervades their body healing appears to speed up. If these individuals can laugh at a situation or even themselves, facing the losses confronting them then the battle is half over. They are on their way to recovery. To laugh at the face of fear, depression and obstacles that appear insurmountable are pretty potent. With laughter their ability to attain the goals set forth in our plan of care appears to be more attainable. What a powerful tool to keep in your arsenal, the simple act of laughing. God created laughter. I know this because God created us. Just sit back and observe how funny we are. It is literally amazing how some people put one foot in front of the other. Laughing should be packaged in a bottle, to be taken at least 4 times per day not necessarily with food, but a good bottle of wine wouldn't hurt. I can tell you were about to chuckle.

Look in the mirror; now again look in the mirror naked. Now that should bring a chuckle or two. You had better either put your clothes back on or shut the lights. You don't want that bladder to give out. Laughing is rather a pretty easy expression for the most part. It is my opinion that laughing should be easier for the senior citizen. Since it takes less muscles to smile than frown and we know everything goes south (our body droops) then laughing should be pretty easy. It is kind of funny that we don't see comedians entertaining in the nursing facility. Rather we see musicians and singers, why? Probably because seniors are a tough audience. Our hearing tends to severely decline with aging. Probably over half of the audience will miss the punch-line because they didn't hear it. They may have fallen asleep. You see that smile can easily turn into laughter, be careful. Don't laugh, take this merry-go-round called life ever so serious. Me, I choose to laugh at myself and the world I live in. This planet is a comedy of errors. Laughing will make you feel better, and I am for that. I am still going to hold onto my day job. Everyone is a critic.

Through the Eyes of a Child

Have you ever just sat still and observed you children, grandchildren or any children play? Watch the interactions with other children. Next time you take your children or any children to the toy store or museum just watch them. Watch their eyes, their expressions and their body language. What I have observed, since my profession teaches me to be very observant of body language, is pure fascination with what they see. Let's put special glasses over our aging eyes and see what they see. The first thing that comes to me is the clarity and acuteness of all that I see. Of course that would be first because as we age we are focusing our attention on the steady decline in our physiology. I don't need the glasses; I can see with crisp, acute, sharp and focused vision. Keep on imagining. The newness of this acute vision is fascinating. I turn my eyes in all directions, so I don't miss anything. I stare momentarily at objects big and small, so the details register in my mind. This clarity of vision is wonderful. The excitement is building to see all the details I've been missing with my aging eyes. I am certainly not taking this new acuteness for granted. I'm enjoying everything my new eyes can take in. A big smile ensues and wonderment is my dominate expression. Amazement, excitement, fascination, joy, and fun begin to overpower my feelings of aging and the decline of my body's organs.

Memories begin to reach my consciousness of days gone by. I remember going shopping with my mother for the upcoming holidays. We were in this toy store and I was running from one toy to another, playing as fast as I could with everything within my grasp. The excitement was overwhelming. There was also that time that my brother took me to a television studio for a Saturday morning kid's program called "Wonderama." We played games and Simon Sez. In fact when I was called out of Simon Sez I walked right in front of the camera as I returned to my seat. I have not thought of that memory for some time.

I remember going to the Museum of Natural History. There was this giant dinosaur that looked so ferocious. I walked through those halls with my mouth and my eyes opened wide in utter amazement. You know these special glasses are pretty good. I am concentrating on every detail of those memories as we continue on this imaginative journey. I remember going to the Polo Grounds to watch my first baseball game. I was walking out of the lobby towards our seats and this field opens up right in front of me. That grass was so green, the dirt was so groomed. The players were all warming up and they looked bigger than life. Wait, there is "Willie Mays" wow, he's fast. I remember going to Yankee Stadium with our school and again the enormousness of the stadium was overwhelming. There was Mickey Mantle in center field, Whitey Ford pitching and Roger Maris in right field. These icons were bigger than life. I traded their baseball cards with my friends. Even though we sat way up I could make out every detail. If I had only held onto those cards now. Isn't that the truth for all the items in our past? The details are becoming clearer as

I focus my attention on them. There is not time to think about my aching knees or difficulty hearing what someone said, or trying to read the labels. It is time to play baseball and that was the center of the universe. What a great day. A smile comes across my face and for a moment I am back at the stadium.

One of the perks of being a physical therapist is you get to know your patients in depth. They share with you concerns that the doctors or nurses usually don't get, because we spend a lot of one on one time with their exercises. I have always felt this is one of the wonderful perks of my profession. So many patients have shared their own memories of yesterday, that my books have evolved from them. This one elderly lady was sharing her memories with me as she related a story of how her father took her to the state fair. With her special glasses of imagination on she recalled to me how her father paid 25 cents (which was a lot of money at that time) so she could take a ride in a biplane. The look and expression on her face was priceless. The smile and excitement was spreading rapidly as she was telling me this story. She went on to tell me that the pilot was a young man named "Charles

Lindbergh." Can you imagine that, she took a ride with history.

Stop reading the memo's for a moment, and put your imaginative glasses on and return to yesteryear as you recall looking at it, through the eyes of a child. The amazement, fascination, joy, fun, marvel, astonishment, indescribable, flabbergast, with the utter joy of wonderment and awe you interact with a gapping mouth wide open and eyes bulging to see all there is and you are aghast with excitement. Maybe that is what the meaning from the scriptures is telling us. To enter heaven it must be through the eyes of a child. This region of spirituality does not encompass limitations that the physical and emotional regions do. Here you are whatever you choose. In fact you don't need any special imaginative glasses. Your eyes are perfect. You see, your perception is not limited by age or aging. Maybe your thoughts are and your physical is, but not in the spiritual region.

Here God's image prevails upon you. In God's image we are. It's here where, as the Movie says, "What Dreams May Come" starring Robin Williams and Cuba Gooding Jr. You don't have to leave this earth to experience it. At first just put your imaginative glasses on and perceive your experiences through the eyes of a child. Your perception is your reality. From this region the physical and emotional region follows as it reaches back up to the spiritual region as we go through this life. Let no one tell you what you can imagine, recall, or think about. God gave us that gift of free will. You can use it; it is your birth right. Your perception is just that yours. Let those imaginative glasses fly like the wind. As the expression goes "the sky is the limit." Actually there are no limitations unless you choose to have them. Again, your perceptions are your reality. Keep looking around through the eyes of a child. Stop reading the memos. You are again to repeat myself, created in the image of God by God. So let the perception fly freely and choose wisely. Your perceptions make up your reality. As Napoleon Hill stated in his book *Think and Grow Rich* "*what the mind of man can conceive and believe, he will achieve," not only in the physical region or emotional region but naturally in the spiritual region. Conceive and believe through the eyes of a child with all of its amazements and you will achieve.*

Knowledge Is Power

**God Grant us the SERENITY to accept the
things we cannot change;
The COURAGE to change the things we can;
And the WISDOM to know the difference.
What we could never do alone ~
We can do together.
One day at a time ~
One step at a time.**

Is power being 6 feet tall and 250 pounds, built
for the sport of football, strong and lean but
very muscular with a keen sense of martial arts
and a clear understanding of guns, trained in
the special forces and served his country in
a combat zone? One, would you pick a fight
with this person, and two, is this individual

powerful? The answer is obviously yes from a physical perspective and probably from an emotional perspective as well. Is power being 5 feet 8 inches tall and 145 pounds, built like a computer technician, short and thin kind of brainy looking with a keen sense of the legal system and served his country for a long time as a supreme court justice. One, would you pick a fight with this person, and two, is this individual powerful? The answer is not so obvious with the second person. However, the answer is most infallibly yes. In fact the second individual is so powerful that his decisions affect all Americans. The first individual is powerful from a physical perception, and you would want him on your side in any conflict. But the second person speaks and the nation listens. He has told many Presidents of the United States where to go and how to do it. His opinions affect our lives and our future. In both examples power came to mind. Physical power where strength, wit and taught skills, empowered that individual to possess this power. With the second person the power that individual demonstrates comes from education, appointment to the Supreme Court of the United States, and knowledge of the law. From that person's experiences "wisdom" was growing. His knowledge was power even though this person was not muscular, not trained in the martial arts and guns. This person exuded power. This person was addressed as "your honor." Great leaders from around the world would dine and converse with him. The President of the United States would humbly listen to him. Now that is power when the most powerful person in the world, the President of the United States, would listen and at times he explained the interpretation of the law of the land.

Knowledge is power and so is physical strength. An interesting thing happens when you get older. You get weaker. The reflexes slow down, the steadiness of holding a gun starts to shake. On the other hand as the Supreme Court Justice ages, he is getting wiser and smarter. His knowledge of the laws and their interpretations are growing in fairness of decisions, and experiences. His knowledge is growing as is his judgment because of the many that cross the Supreme Court justices desk.

What can a person due with this knowledge? The younger stronger man, a very brave individual, will defend our country and give his life to save us from tyranny and anyone trying to attack us.. The second person through his knowledge of the law was appointed to the Supreme Court. Knowledge can be applied to both an emotional and physical perspective. Both avenues are extremely important. I send a large thank you to all our soldiers who have defended us and protected us against any harmful threats. To all our soldiers past and present this writer extends a hearty thank you for your service.

Have you ever experienced an individual who brags about how good they are at what they do. In fact these individuals are knowledgeable on most every subject. They appear to be experts in most everything. Then there is the Supreme Court justice who is a very quiet, confident individual, who had power coming out of his body. You just knew when he spoke everyone listened. I have previously suggested that as we get older we get wiser, and more knowledgeable about life's experiences.

These experiences provide wisdom and a subtle quiet confident inner strength is felt. His accrued knowledge is powerful. His education made him strong. The first individual will lose his strength as the years go on. But the second individual will only get more powerful, as the years go by. This will continue to grow in all of us if we don't block the process. There are many ways, as we age, we block this knowledge and power from growing:

(1) We choose to stop learning. (2) We accept the preconceived parameters, others have placed on us. (3) We believe, in all our cells, that we can not do anything more. (4) We believe there are obvious limitations in what we can accomplish. (5) We are old and feeble in both our physical and emotional regions. (6) We believe there is no hope to change anything about ourselves. (7) We believe we are just a burden to society because we are old and not working anymore. (8) We believe it is impossible to do any of the things I have mentioned in this book because we can hardly see, along with other physical limitations. (9) We believe that all we are is the physical and emotional being. (10) We believe the spiritual being is something that might happen after death, or may not. (11) We believe what you see is what we are, and (12) we are skeptical about all that has been written in this book. It sounds good, but it falls in the fiction category along with "Star Wars and Star Trek." The only power one has is their bank account, how many toys they have accumulated, and their

physical health. This pretty much summarizes some popular beliefs regarding how we can block the fact that knowledge is power.

Hold onto these perceived notions and one will definitely stay stuck in their perceptions of how powerless they really are because they are old. The skeptics, who write those memos will win and keep you safely categorized as an expenditure to society and basically a burden. Thoughts like, "I wish God will take me now," "I am such a burden to my family", "life is just hopeless", "I am so alone," now this perceived attitude is not one of power. Let us look at the previous blocks to accruing knowledge and subsequent power.

Earlier I asked you to use that great gift of imagination through the eyes of a child. Please put on those magical glasses and look around. Now put in your ears a magical device that allows you to "be still and know that I am." Be still and listen, God the almighty is communicating with you. You are In God's presence. Quiet your inner voice, be still, listen to the powerful insights that are coming to your awareness. Focus on that and through the magical glasses and hearing device we can listen and hear, see and visualize, regardless of our age, lot in life, educational attainments, diplomas, wealth, or where we are residing on this planet.

These are the blocks to knowledge and power; (1) We choose to stop learning. This one is quite simple. Keep your mind open to all that is around you. Focus your attention on details like drinking a fine wine. Do not just gulp it down; keep it in your mouth a little longer. Focus on the flavors you are experiencing. Start the day with the idea of "today I will learn something new" With all the millions of information bits traveling up and down your spinal cord and reaching your brain, you are learning constantly to restore functions, adapt to the environment, or compensate. This physiological process is always running. Realize it and go forth for today is the first day of the rest of your life. (2) We accept the preconceived parameters, others have placed on us. This one is also simple. Stop reading the memos. Just choose to only accept what "You" accept as the parameters. Keep practicing this thought, and if enough of it keeps registering on your brain patterns, some of it will stick. (3) We believe, in all our cells, that we can not do anything more. This one requires a slight shift of interpretations. You know beyond a shadow of any doubt that the sun is going to rise in the east tomorrow. Now take that 100% conviction and add some process from the physical region. For example, I know that my heart will keep beating in the next hour. Now it might stop but if I don't have a medical history of advanced heart disease there is a 95% chance it will keep beating, not a 100% but close. You have the capability to learn a new skill regardless of your age. The expression goes that we are only using about 10% of our brain capacity. That means we have a "Hard drive" that has a 90% unused space. Read, do brain exercises, learn some new, challenging skill. Learn to speak a new language. Go take a course, given by our community colleges, on any new subject you want. Get a computer and search the internet. Volunteer, to be a mentor to a younger person. (4) We believe there are obvious limitations in what we can accomplish. Just read the accomplishments previous people have done. Read about, Helen Keller, Franklin D Roosevelt, Thomas Edison, Abraham Lincoln. In fact go to the library or on line and read about anyone who was faced with obstacles, and laughed at it and forged ahead. They did not take no for an answer. Maybe that was you in your younger days. Remember what the mind of man can conceive and believe he will achieve. Speak to an athlete at the beginning of the season. Their confidence in winning is a given. (5) We are old and feeble in both our physical and emotional regions. Just read my books. We are more than the physical and emotional states. We have the potential to learn all about the spiritual region. We have free will to choose what we want to digest and accept as our belief system. And of course we can change our perception and choose another. (6) We believe there is no hope to change anything about ourselves. Look at a copy of Life magazines end of year issue, and the issue on the 20th century. Change defined the 20th century in every aspect of our existence. Just over a 100 years ago, there was no airplane, electric stove, refrigerator, air conditioners, automobiles, antibiotics, organ transplants, space exploration, and of course no Velcro. (7) We believe we are just a burden to society because we are old and not working anymore. Well this age group (retirees) are still paying taxes in the services rendered to them. Our seniors are paying taxes on their social security benefits. And my generation (baby boomers) which will be the largest portion, will be a great contributor to society. Our buying power, services needed, savings accounts, investments, will be an asset instead of a deficit. The next generation will be banking on this need for their services as we age.

The medical industry is at the forefront of current events. The cost is sky rocketing. That is not a deficit but income for our next generation. (8) We believe it is impossible to do any of the things I have mentioned in this book because we can hardly see, along with other physical limitations. Our government is considering raising the retirement age, probably to keep those people paying taxes. So many children are returning home because they are having financial problems. So many grandparents are raising their grandchildren. Statistics tells us that as we age a change in our careers is highly likely to occur. Some of recent presidents were well into their senior years. Modern technology has addressed the physical limitations by developing new technology. GPS guidance systems are better than the old way of asking for directions. Those units can pinpoint where you are to the foot. It also will direct you to any direction you request. (9) We believe that all we are is the physical and emotional being. This one takes faith and belief in your own unique relationship with God. Within the physical there are limitations to the range of sound our ears can hear. Does that mean that those higher and lower frequencies do not exist? The microscope and the electron microscope opened up a new world living on the surface of our arm. Because we can't see or hear doesn't mean is doesn't exist. As far as your emotional limitations look outside the box. Most limitations are self imposed. (10) We believe the spiritual being is something that might happen after death or it might not. Talk to people who have experienced the "Near Death" experience. (11) We believe what you see is what you get. David took down Goliath. Talk to your parents and the countless sacrifices they made. They will tell you "I don't know how we did it" Upon looking back what we saw seemed unattainable such as the United States Hockey team that defeated the Russian team in 1980, the Miracle New York Mets of 1969, my grandfather coming to America with nothing and building a very successful business that supported many family and allowed my uncle to retire in his fifties. (12) We are skeptical about all that has been written in this book. Skepticism is a good protector at times. Re-Read the book; look at the facts, and make your decisions on knowledge. That knowledge is power.

And Now the Skeptics Speak

It is not bad to be skeptical. In fact being skeptical can save you a lot of money and emotional aggravation. Skepticism, doubt and distrust are not negative programs. I would consider them assets. One of the side effects of a free capitalistic society is how many con artists, come out of the woodwork to attempt to steal your hard earned money and your good name. Greed is a side effect of a free capitalistic society. These people wait and then attack with full armaments. The sad thing is that the statistic of people being conned is in epidemic proportion. The professionals at the banks, stock markets, grocery stores and department stores, are trying to stay one step ahead. Look at all the security we have to go through.

The elderly are particularly prone to secret questions, passwords, and identity protection. There are evil people. So as you read my book, hold onto your skepticism. Your life's experiences provide you with the experience to make safe judgments. I do believe what you do onto others usually gets done onto you. There is always someone richer/poorer than you to the right and always someone poorer/richer than you to the left. Money by itself is not evil. It is inert. A $100 dollar bill lying on the floor has no power, can't do anything, until someone picks it up and moves it around (shopping, or investing). Let's put on a table the most recent miracle drug. Taking this medicine will cure the worst disease one can imagine. So place this drug on the table and leave it alone. What will happen to that specific disease you are supposed to take this miracle drug for? Well left on the table NOTHING. It has to be ingested into your body to work its miracle. I am stating the obvious but I am trying to make a point. The same analogy occurs when you find a great book. The words inside this book can help you improve your life. But if you do not pick the book up and read it, then like the miracle drug nothing will happen. The medicine has to be digested and the words have to be digested.

One of many great things God has put into you is a basic program to survive. These elementary programs seed more complicated programs. I said from the beginning that the words in this book are food for thought. You can go a short while without food or water, but not too long. We call this program, instincts. I would like the reader to digest these words and take from them what you need. The choices are always your free will to make. I am not asking anyone to follow any particular belief the tenets of which are so diverse and complicated we need our Rabbi's, Priests, Fathers, and Ministers to interpret the individual nuances.

The how to I leave in their well qualified abilities. So hold onto your skepticism and question the words in this book. A true skeptic might argue the point that if God makes no junk and from the spiritual region is total harmonic balance then why are bad things happening to good people. Why are there diseases, killing and a world on the brink of one potential disaster after another? Why is famine and poor living conditions present? Why does human kind suffer and still maintain a kill or be killed attitude towards their fellow human. What is life - as Mark Twain said, "life is nothing but one damned thing after another"? Why is such a large part of the inhabitants of this planet living on the brink of starvation, poverty, pain, anguish and dying at such a young age? Why are the majority of senior citizens having a tough time surviving? Why are our senior citizens treated as second class citizens? Why is there disease, killing, hatred, jealousy, and evil on a beautiful green/blue planet.

I remember listening to one of the astronauts describing Earth from outer space. I recall how the astronaut described how the differences of opinions and lifestyles were not visible from space. All he saw was a beautiful green/blue planet, effortlessly turning in the vast realm of the universe. God creates no junk, so what's happening. I have to quote a line from the movie "Rudy" a story about perseverance, and hope of a short minimal athletic skilled individual whose dream was to go to Notre Dame and not only go to the College but play football for them. This 5 foot 8 inch individual did not stop there. He wanted to play at least one down of a regular season. Well miracles are there for the taking. This individual not only graduated from Notre Dame, but played football for 4 years on the practice squad and did play in one game. As the story goes he was the only player to date to be carried off the field on his teammates shoulders. Well, the line in the movie goes like this; Rudy is talking to a Priest and asking for advice on how to get into the school. Rudy is pleading with the Priest to help him get in. The priest tells Rudy the following, "I have learned two things in my life (1) there is a God, and (2) I am not him. Another great line was from the movie "Evan Almighty" God masquerading as a waiter explains to Evan's wife, "God does not give you courage, but the opportunity to demonstrate it God does not give you the money but the opportunity to earn it. God does not just give you a fish to eat for today, but the opportunity to learn how too fish, so you can feed your family for a lifetime. Those are great lines to think about. I present to you words that if digested and utilized present food for thoughts. Those thoughts from the various regions (physical, emotional, and spiritual) guide you through life.

All these adventures and experiences contribute to your perceptions. It is these choices, and one's perception that contribute to your reality. Preconceived notions about the aging process are formulated from many aspects. It is this writer's viewpoint that God created man in his image and that image encompasses omnipotent, omnipresence and omni essence. We are not alone, but part of this grandeur of the creative process in motion. This creation called humans has yet to even approach its full potential. It is my opinion that we are in the infancy stages when it comes to our human health potential. It is that free will that allows us to choose how we want to go through this adventure call life. We are in a constant stage of adapting and compensating to experiences that cross our path's. What I have presented here are tools and a way to view those experiences. The choice is yours so choose wisely.

Conclusion

Our journey for now you may think is coming to an end but in actuality we are just beginning. On this journey I have introduced you to viewpoints about the aging process through a different set of eyes. We explored the aging process from a different point of view. I introduced a concept of the triangle of life. The three components of life are the physical, the emotional and the spiritual. These three components are the basic programs inside you and me. We attempt to live a life of balance amongst the three regions. These regions are all connected and communicating with each other. There is an imbalance where the physical is given predominance. The emotional component adds the zest to the physical. Unfortunately the spiritual region is usually not thought of until we start approaching our mortality. We continued our adventure of thinking beyond the limits set down by others. Our limitations were essentially unlimited. Our limitations were limited by our own imagination. Our presumption was what the Priest told Rudy in the movie "Rudy" what I have learned is one; there is a God and two; I am not him. I do not claim to have the answers to each individual's dilemma. I don't know completely why bad things happen to good people. I do realize there are great forces working on our planet. I have observed over my 33 years in the Medical Profession that some people demonstrated "miraculous" responses and others did not. I have also observed preconceived attitudes, judgments and opinions that are not exactly correct regarding the aging process and our elderly. We are assured of the fact that the aging process will proceed in you and me whether you want it to or not.

I have found that words are very powerful. Our communication amongst ourselves is through words. One's opinion is made up of words, attitudes and viewpoints about the aging process and the elderly are words. The accumulation of these words is power. This power is not necessarily might and brawn. The quiet confidence of knowledge is exuded by many of the patients I have had the privilege of working with. These individuals did not possess special powers other than the motivation to be all that they can be. Together we forged ahead breaking down traditional notions of what the elderly can or can not do.

We dissected these preconceived ideas and found that the aging process allows us to expand our assets. For example the emotions of laughter, trust, wisdom, knowledge are not lost as we age but enhanced. Our elderly are to be honored, respected, and held in a place of achievement in our society. This elder generation led this nation through a difficult 20th century. What our elders have witnessed in achievements is remarkable such as the many wars that at a time looked bleak for our country. It appears that throughout our history a great leader came forth and guided us through the darkness. Our country is truly blessed and the words "One nation under God" rings loud and clear. Words are powerful tools and we use them on a daily basis. These powerful words are not to be taken for granted. It is by the grace of God that we live in a country called the United States of America. A melting pot of every nationality, race or creed living in one country. We are to honor and respect the elderly because as I have given concepts to ponder, they have earned it. I have written some personal stories with permission from my patients. These brave people have shared their experiences and food for thought about some of the tough issues our elderly are going through. If the inner voice inside your head constantly bombards the brain with words like I am old and feeble, hopeless, lonely, sad, discouraged, and just plain noncontributory to society. No wonder they ask God to take them. God gives us the gifts of life and free will to choose how one wants to travel the roads of life. Many people have read the memos that tell one how to believe, what to believe, and whom to believe.

Stop reading the memos. You have over 8 billion brain cells with unlimited connections and variations and interpretations as unlimited as your imagination will allow. It appears from observing the evening news that we are still stuck in a very low setting. If you are a "Star Trek" fan that may be the reason the Federation of Planets has not exposed themselves to us. The science fiction writers are not that far from the truth/reality and this reality is your perception.

Choose your perceptions and your reality will follow. A group exerts its influence on others with a perceived reality that encompasses their surrounding world. When Christopher Columbus sailed the perceived reality held true to their thinking that the world was square and the three little ships were going to fall off the face of the earth. Well that didn't happen. From the lines of the movie "Rudy", I have learned two things (1) there is a God and (2) I am not him. Yet God created man in his image with God being omnipotent, omnipresence and omni essence. Then we are God's creations have elements of those characteristics in us. Looking at the history of humankind you would think quite the opposite. This is where our elderly population is a great asset and not a great expenditure. Their knowledge and experiences and subsequent acquired wisdom raises them above this low level of Cain killing Abel, to a higher level of spirituality within God's image of us. Now let these words of hope, possibilities, encouragement, wisdom, laughter, trust and unconditional love perfused through all of your 45 quadrillion cells on a daily basis from birth to death.

The quiet strength, confidence and connection with the almighty is so ingrained in your existence that I defy any virus, bacterium, mold or negative thought to take hold. You are in a space with God, protected and loved by God. The possibilities are unlimited. Truly the green/blue planet observed from space is the same on the surface as it is viewed from outer space. The knowledge our elderly have accrued is priceless. This clear understanding makes our elderly an asset to be utilized. They are such an important part of our country. Their contributions have not begun to be used. I sure can use the wisdom my Grandfather accrued. It behooves one generation to utilize these assets before that generation becomes the elderly.

To now return to the title of this book "What is so Good about Getting older." If you cannot come to the conclusion that everything is good about getting older then I suggest you re read the words I have put on these pages. Do not limit your judgments by just the physical or emotional regions. Utilize all points of the triangle. With words being so powerful, choose wisely the words you will allow to repeat in your brain. It is possible to change. For one thing realize that it is possible. Your ability to restore old viewpoints, compensate or adapt is part of your basic program if you have to put those magical glasses on and view your surroundings through the eyes of a child.

Age has passed on those achievements and perceptions to the next generation. As they age their wisdom and experiences will be passed on. We are nothing short of miraculous created by God in God's image being the root for imagination. Let your imagination fly freely and seed the creations for you as you journey through this life. Open your eyes and look around. Through the eyes of a child what do you see? You are not limited by anything. So next time you meet an elderly individual, keep in mind the millions of cells that make up each of their organs, the millions of messages going up and down their spinal cord, the millions of bits of memory stored in their brain have endless functions operating, for the most part, successfully to allow them to attain senior citizen privileges. Now the honor, respect, admiration and a deep sense of gratitude will automatically come forth. The old perception that the elderly are expenditures will just fade away. Our elderly are assets and nothing short of a potential to be opened and not discarded.

About the Author

Dr Ronald G Sherman has been in the Medical Profession for over 33 years as both a practicing Physical Therapist and Chiropractor. He has had the privilege of working with the elderly achieve great results. These individuals are ordinary people who have shared their experiences, and their thoughts on getting older. Their wisdom has inspired Dr Sherman to write this book in hopes of giving the reader a perspective on the aging population that will lead to a feeling of deep respect and honor for our elderly.